To Jessica!
Thanks
for being
special for
my grandson
one very special!

Rightfully Hers

Beverley
July 5, 2021

Beverley Clarkson

BURKWOOD
Media Group

Burkwood Media Group
P O Box 29448
Charlotte, NC 28229
www.burkwoodmedia.com

ISBN: 978-0-578-65960-2

Printed in the United States of America

Dedication

This book is dedicated to my mother, Daphne, who survived a cruel, loveless childhood. As a youngster, she often begged to die, but thankfully, did not. Despite the tragedy of her childhood, she made a conscious and courageous choice to show her children what love should feel like and look like.

I am further indebted to my brothers and sisters, who took this journey with me. Our oldest brother Orlando died in 1999. He always stood by our mother and me in our new life in America. Talented, full of humor and excitement, he was there to make our lives better.

Preface

I was a child when my mother taught me the invaluable art of listening. The sound of her voice became the essential connection of our lives together. As she read her story to me, I became keenly aware of the sounds in my world: the soft sound of my mother's voice, as she pulled tissue from her pocket and began reading pages from her journal; the soothing sound of leaves from the great Maple as they rustled against her bedroom window during that special time; the mildly annoying sound of my siblings competing for attention downstairs; the sound of my father hollering "D," when he walked through the front door; the symphony of sounds while dinner was being prepared; and then the complete absence of it, a stillness, that enveloped the house when we all went to bed, while the sounds in my head were still active.

I didn't know of any other mothers actually writing, or fathers for that matter. I do remember my father handwriting his sermons in a flowery handwriting style, that I could not read. He was a minister, studying Divinity as a part-time student at

Butler University. His writings were based on biblical doctrine applied to everyday life. I also remember him writing scathing 'Letters to the Editor,' about the civil rights movement, to which our family sometimes received threatening phone calls or hate mail. That made me very nervous. My father never bothered to share his articles with the family. They just appeared mysteriously in the local newspaper. I can still see the smile on his face, satisfied that he was speaking up.

My mother's stories were, however, about her life, a life lived. As it seemed to me at the time, I could readily relate to what she was saying. I laid back comfortably on her bed and imagined her life as she read it to me. I could actually feel the hatred that resonated from her aunt, signifying she was nothing; or feel the tenderness surrounding her from the love of her little cousins. I swallowed my heart when I realized that my grandmother didn't want her own daughter either.

As I listened to my mother read from her journal, I learned that words meant something. They were powerful. Words could help you reconcile what became of your life, or they could reduce you to the lowest common denominator, devastating you, beyond measure.

My mother demonstrated through her writings that you can actually relive your life through words: face your fears, embrace your happiness, put the wretchedness behind you, share your secrets, and bring your life into the sunshine, no matter how beautiful or painful. Each of us can do this. I learned life lessons from listening to my mother, and in turn, I supported her efforts to reconcile the pain in her own life.

Chapter 1

I watched my mother's reflections in the large dresser mirror of her bedroom. Her dresser was about five feet long, in a contemporary style. The cabinet had silver metal pulls that looked quite pronounced against its shiny mahogany surface. It was amazing to me that the drawers were not typically, flat. I supposed the wood was soaked in water over time in a vat to get this result, because each drawer had a wide rolling facade. Really neat, and there were several of them. I ran my fingers across the wavy fronts. The mirror was the full length of the dresser.

Night after night, (my father at his second job), my mother wrote in a journal she called, "My Life Story." While she wrote, I tried on her jewelry, and patted face powder on my cheek, rubbing it in to blend with my darker complexion. And yes, I sprayed her perfume behind my ear and on my inner wrist, the pulse points - she told me, as I had seen my mother do. Her favorite was Chanel #5. I was ten years old at the time.

My mother kept her costume jewelry (bargain basement finds she called them) in a large drawer at the top of her dresser. I fingered popcorn pearls in all colors, lifted mounds of gold chains, rhinestone necklaces and earrings, pulled vintage pendants out of this entanglement, while my mother was dedicated to those memories. A number of times, I watched her pull a handkerchief from her chenille robe pocket and dab a tear away.

Every now and then, my mother looked up, seeing my face in the beveled edge glass, she smiled at me; I smiled back. There was no need for me to turn around to face her, because we could see each other's reflection clearly in the mirror, which left no room for privacy. We were together, but separate. No words spoken between us.

I really liked this time with my mother, just the two of us. Quiet and peaceful! My three younger siblings bathed and asleep, my brother Norman (one year older) watching television downstairs in the living room and my oldest brother Orlando (5 years older) talking to his girlfriend while seated on the retro telephone bench in the dining room.

This time was special. I adored seeing our everyday lives reflected in the large mirrored vanity; and the bright colors in my parent's room captivated me, not the soft pinks that were in my room, the girls' room.

***

Months before, my mother told me why she was writing about her life: Our family doctor suggested that she write her childhood story, in hopes that recalling these memories could offset her struggles with depression. I looked up this word in our encyclopedia, but I didn't see how this applied to my mother. I never saw signs of depression, this monster that captured her soul. Granted, I was a child, but it did not manifest itself in my interactions with her, nor with my brothers and sisters. She was always cheerful, willing to play games with us, and ready to talk, laugh and read with her children. My neighborhood friends came by, hoping my mother was home, so they could laugh with her too. They loved to talk with her.

Yet depression was there, something deep inside of her that I could not see. This journal was possibly forty years too late for my mother, but timely for me. She shared with me, a foreboding thought that penetrated her daily life - *she would not live to see her children grow up.* And because her own childhood was so horrible, she feared that in her absence, our lives would be deplorable too.

***

Each time my mother wrote, she cried, pulled a hankie or tissue from her robe pocket, and held the white crushed material in her hand. When finished for the night, she placed the three-ring pages of her red and white binder in her mahogany bookcase headboard, then slid it shut.

Finally, the day arrived, and she was anxious to read her story out loud to me. I must admit that when my mother was at work, and Orlando was out with his friends, Norman and I pulled out her journal to see what she was writing. What was the secret, after all? Typical children! We never told her this of course, as this would certainly be a breach of privacy. However, because she told me her story many times over the years, I thought a sneak peek would be okay.

***

When I sat on her bed that day, the feathered pillows flattened immediately as my head rested against the starchy white pillowcases.

My mother's voice was pleasant, yet there was something in its resonance when she read from "My Life's Story," that I could not really place. I was a little nervous, not sure why – I knew her story well – but I was. Possibly, it was her return to that destitute place and time. My thinking was that it would be a harrowing experience, the second encounter just as bad or worse than the initial events.

Her hand embraced a hankie, that she removed from her Muumuu (a popular house dress in the fifties). I recognized my father's monogrammed white handkerchief. In anticipation, because there were no tears yet, my mother clutched the cotton fabric for dear life – the life she lost perhaps – the life that haunted her still. Taking a deep breath, my mother, Daphne, began.

"Nearly all stories start with 'Once upon a time;' but this one I would like to start just a little differently. So, I think I will say, 'It must have been a beautiful day when I was born. They told me, it was two p.m. on Tuesday afternoon, the 18th of January, 1922....'"

I smiled to myself, 'Yes, a beautiful day, like this one perhaps,' and felt an immediate connection to the childhood stories as mother read aloud. They always started with, "Once upon a time." Our favorites, we begged my mother to read over and over like, "The Emperor Has No Clothes," and "Hansel and Gretel." But this story was not a fairytale, and whether there would be a happy ending was not guaranteed.

As she read, my mind tiptoed to the past. Through the chronicles of my mother's life, I ran with her into the darkness. Holding hands, my heart pounding in my chest and my legs following the path that only my mother could direct. I knew my mother's story, had heard it many times, yet each time was like the first, because of the intimacy between us. This time, however, she wrote it down and was reading it out loud to me. I thought that was remarkable!

I wished I had streamers and blowers to make this day really special, like Times Square on New Year's Eve. In anticipation of her presentation, each day I excitedly wanted to ask her, "Are you ready yet?" But I didn't dare become an annoying brat, echoing my younger brother and sisters, "Are we there yet," on neighborhood trips in the car?

Ironically, in my mind, my mother was living her life, as she precariously and meticulously prepared me for her death. However, I sat comfortably and listened to her gentle voice as the sunshine pushed its way into the bedroom, making abstract shadings on the walls from branches of the Maple tree in our front yard.

"When I say beautiful day, I am thinking about my feelings really. First, I would like to explain

a little about myself. As far back as I can remember, I have always been carefree. I take life as it comes, good or bad, because I think it would have been a lot worst...."

Yes, life was a struggle for Daphne. This fiery red-haired child was born and raised in Jamaica, BWI. I recalled my mother saying to me, "At least I was never molested." But bits and pieces of that child, the one - no one wanted after the deaths of her grandmother and great grandmother (Grandam) - were lost in the dehumanization of her spirit, and the systematic denial of love that was, I believe, RIGHTFULLY HERS.

I felt safe in my mother's presence and understood that she needed me to witness her life unfold, layer by layer. The polished cotton floral bed comforter caught my attention with its intensity of color. The comforter was soft and puffy as the back of my thin legs felt its surface. The heat from the sun on the fabric, reminded me of pulling warm clothing from our electric dryer.

As mother and daughter, we were also friends and confidants, with that special bonding that comes from love without conditions providing a basis for intuition that can't be explained.

When the wind blew, maple leaves, the size of my hands, gently stroked the window's surface, nudging me with its quiet presence, as my mother read acid accounts of her past.

Stymied by memories, "Little red bastard!... Girl children ain't nothing but shit!" my grandmother screamed at her daughter again and again. Yet, my mother turned head-on to face that child. Daphne made a life for herself. Yet my mother could not turn away from that child. She needed to validate that little girl. Those words spoken by her mother ravished Daphne's soul, like childhood scarlet fever, damaging the delicate vessels of her heart, permanently scarred for a lifetime. The pain of that child still raged within the woman sitting before me.

***

In my mind, I see my grandmother Phyllis with hatred mounting for the life she lost due to the illegitimate birth of her daughter Daphne, my mother. Having come from a well-to-do country family, her father arranged pick up from Phyllis' boarding school, when notified by the administration that she was with child.

"Me suffering," Phyllis cried. "Anyone hear me? Me don't want to live like this! Hidden like some common criminal! I love him, you see, Mommy!"

Her mother angrily said "...From this day forth, YOU DO NOT EXIST! Hear me Child.... You betta' listen good! When that baby comes, it will be taken from you ...Ya thinks a baby can rear a baby?...Me no longer want to see your retched face...."

Phyllis blamed the child within her. The child who wanted everything, but who would bring her nothing!

***

My mother's earthly pleasures and delights were in seeing the joy within her children now, three boys and three girls. The three older children were born in Jamaica and the younger ones, here in the United States.

I was the oldest of the girls and with that position came added responsibilities. My mother wanted everything for her children that she never had; but as an adult, my mother wanted for herself, only shoes, shoes that child never wore and clothes she never had. Shoes to cover her encrusted heels and soles, cushioning her feet on those five-mile hikes to take her aunt's husband his lunch; and real clothing, not the potato gunny sacks she wore as dresses, to obliterate the scratchiness of the jute scouring her skin. The paths were evident – behind her neck, under her arms and on the backs of her legs. A proper dress- was that too much to ask? Yet oddly, I recognized, joy was missing in my mother's perception of her life.

***

It seemed peculiar to me that a family of means, who could well afford to take care of a little child, entrusted her well-being to an aunt who wanted nothing to do with her. Resented her in fact, hated her and provided her nothing in common comfort and expectations, because she was a bastard child.

***

"My childhood days as it seemed passed on quickly. It was rough, or I should say 'real rugged.'

My great grandmother died, also my grandmother, who I understand was my real back bone. I was about three or four years old. In those days in the country, when someone dies, ice was placed around them. There were no funeral homes. The body was kept at home. Friends, neighbors and relatives would come and stay, sometimes for days with the family.

Well, my grandmother died one night. I guess I was asleep, because the next day, there were a lot of people coming and going.... I was told my grandmother had died, but I didn't understand. Not seeing her out as usual, I went to her room."

I remembered that room. My grandmother, Phyllis, described that room to me, and that memory flooded my mind. The house was in the Jamaican countryside, far into the Blueridge Mountains, near an old slavery town. The neighbors were paupers. But this one house stood out, rich on bauxite red beaming soil. The logs basted in the confines of thick vegetation, like the skin of its human inhabitants glowing beautifully in the sun.

Highly polished oak floors supported hand-crafted African-mahogany and ebony furniture. The bed had four tall, heavy, mahogany posts, intricately hand-carved with flowers and leaves, as were the other furniture pieces. Every other day the pieces were polished with linseed oil and bee's wax to help withstand the penetrating heat and drenching rains.

***

The emotional strength my mother thought she didn't have in her constitution, although it was always present, she found in me. She shared with me her fears, her hopes for all her children, her pain, her disappointment in marriage, which was certainly impacted by a five-year separation as my father traveled to England, Panama, and America. And because my mother left her homeland, Jamaica, and came to a new home in America, she had few friends in Indianapolis, Indiana. My father selected this city because he was enrolled as a part-time divinity student at Butler University, so I was her friend.

My mother, Daphne, prepared me from an early age to step in and provide the support my younger brother and sisters would need. She even wanted me to make sure that my father was supported with his breakfast, dinner, clothes washed and ironed, and the house cleaned. I did not get along with my father. He believed that children should be seen and not heard.

I was always angry with my father as he was with me. He didn't like that I challenged him, questioned his thinking. I wasn't belligerent, but I was definitely quietly defiant. I only yelled at him when he refused to listen. He was always so confident that his way was the right and only way. It became my wake-up call, "I hate you! I hate you!" I would yell as I ran up the stairs when he made me angry. I was alive!

My father's dominating presence in our home overwhelmed us when he was there. He personified the Jamaican ethos, "One job man? Cha mon, ya' lazy." He always had two or three jobs. Every weekend, his white-glove test determined if we met his cleaning standards; other than that, he expected his children to be only seen.

Yes, my mother really believed she would not survive. Her thoughts were pure and honest. I believed she would, though. I had to believe that. I watched her every day as a child, and she seemed well to me. No indicators of illness. I believed my father was the trigger. They argued frequently, my mother having to defend herself. I did not want to do anything extra for my father, other than being a good student.

One argument my parents had was based on what you could say my father's principles. He said, "Daphne you cannot put beer in my refrigerator. I am a minister."

My mother replied, "What do you mean YOUR refrigerator. This refrigerator belongs to the family."

My father then tried to use his ministerial approach, "Daphne you must be reasonable. I am a 'man of the cloth.' What would people say or think?"

My mother studied him, dark eyes intense, waited, then said confidently, "I don't give a damn what they think," and she walked out of the kitchen. My father stood there believing that he had the last word; satisfaction plastered on his face. Orlando, Norman and I did not move.

At the end of the month, my mother ordered a new refrigerator. They moved my father's refrigerator out.

Numerous times my parents' arguments would escalate out-of-control with pushing and shoving. On one time, I remember my mother grabbing the black cast iron skillet with bacon oil from our morning breakfast to defend herself.

Orlando ran to the basement to hide our father's shotgun, not sure if he would try to kill our mother or all of us. The rusty gun, from when the basement flooded, was as tall as me, but sturdy and heavy. Norman and I followed Orlando serving as lookouts in the event our father decided it was time. I was so nervous. My heart was heavy in my thin chest, with my breathing. I could see and feel my chest moving up and down rapidly. Luckily, it never came to that.

I was cautious of those whom my mother said hurt her, knowing that her childhood experiences were beyond repair.

My mother shared with me comments she heard as a child. "I (Daphne) stood up and quietly closed the mesh door behind me. I heard my aunt and uncle talking. 'Me no pay for no school for that girl. She worthless anyway, a bastard child.'"

"My chest tightened, and my breathing quickened, as 'worthless and bastard' weighed down me skinny chest and crushed my heart. I held my breath, did not move or I would be chastised for listening in on 'grown people's talk....'"

"Me tel'la ya, that girl lazy, ya see!" her aunt continued.

I would in time get to know my maternal grandmother, Phyllis. My mother encouraged me to write letters to her in Jamaica. She became my pen-pal. I looked forward to getting those letters. My mother never corresponded with her mean aunt, whom she lived with, once she left her house, nor the little cousins, whom she loved. It was clear that chapter in her book was closed.

My mother's relationship with my father was a source of her disappointments; but her relationship with my grandmother was a reservoir of never-ending pain, drowning her in despair. Deeply rooted in her childhood, she held on to any branch she could find to keep from flowing out to sea with the other hatchlings, following the massive tortoises, their mothers.

***

I noticed an intensity behind my mother's eyes as she read. I felt a little hot, so I shifted my body to get more air from the window fan.

"No one was in the room, but my grandmother. She was lying on the bed, but strangely, her jaws were tied with a white rag. I did my best to wake her. 'Grandmother,' I whispered. "Grandmother, what's wrong?" I spoke louder this time; but she didn't answer. I spoke one more time to wake her. 'Grandmother.' I could barely get the words out

when a hand grabbed my shoulders. Someone had entered the room. I didn't even hear the person come in. Startled I looked into the eyes of the person."

'What you doing here, child?'

"I didn't have a chance to answer. I was taken out."

I couldn't imagine why anyone would frighten a child like that. She was only looking for her grandmother; death holds such mystery. My mother was just ushered out, without explanation.

"She was buried the next day in the family plot, not far from the house. As I remember now, I used to sit on her grave talking and hoping one day that she would return.

Well, it was not the end of the world. I still had a home and family, but I did not know a real mother or father. As time passed, my great grandmother who was in bed and could not move unless someone helped her, and I became close. I would help her all I could. I even helped her use the bedpan; and oddly today, I can still hear her *voice saying, 'God bless you my child,' as she patted me on the head."*

My mother looked up. Her eyes were no longer on the paper she was reading from. It was as if the words she was reading were memorized, already in her head, permanently implanted in the cast of her brain.

I couldn't believe it at the time. All the words Norman and I read while my mother was at work, were pouring out of her mouth, and she was not looking at the paper.

"I know today that some of her blessings are still with me, because I was so small, and even the relatives used to wonder how I could have helped her so much. Now I know that it was not 'little ole me,' but God was with me and he gave me strength.

When I was about five years old, she died. I knew then that she would not come back, because they buried her alongside my grandmother. I still visited their graves and I would tell them everything, just as if they were alive. When my feelings were hurt, I ran to the graves and cried.

I knew that little girl well, from my mother telling me about her life. I watched, silently yet carefully, in the rear-view mirror of my mind, wanting to reassure that little girl. So much sadness! So many tears! Much too much for one so small!

My mother blotted dampness from her forehead with a rumpled handkerchief. She looked around, focused on me, and smiled. I smiled back, feeling quite comforted, secure in her presence. Mother's voice was soft, and I felt soothed by its sound, like a lullaby.

"It seems funny now, but I always hear my great grandmother's gentle voice saying, 'God bless you my child.' The words didn't mean much then. I didn't really know what she meant, but I knew it was good and the words seemed to be comforting, somehow or other."

When my mother said those words, "God Bless you my child," I knew they held a special meaning for her, even though she did not know the meaning at the time; but the words connected with her over a lifetime to her great grandmother. I could see it in her eyes. That yearning for affection, and the person who was the source of that love, was actually bedridden. My mother probably did not know that she extended her great grandmother's life as well. The two were in need of each other, inseparable.

Perspiration appeared on my mother's brow again, as I looked deeply into the eyes of that child. Bright, shiny brown eyes peered from behind a yellow freckled face. I could see the light within the heart of that child, knowing she was needed, appreciated and was indeed loved.

"Now my life story begins. With my two grandparents gone home to rest, I was a problem and a big one too. The problem was that there were very few married women in my family. It was nearly all men. There were three granduncles, two were married and lived in the same district. There were two other grand uncles. They lived in Cuba and were like strangers, because they never even wrote to the family. There was one aunt and one aunt-in-law. Those were the only two women I knew as relatives. There were others, but I never knew their connection to our family. One grand uncle had three sons, the other had five girls and two boys. My other grand uncle never married but had six boys and two girls. My aunt was single, so she was picked to take care of me.

The only problem was − she didn't want the responsibility, because she wasn't my mother. Well, she moved in with her stepmother and another sister. At the time, her stepmother worked in town or I should say Kingston, the capital of

Jamaica. She would come home and stay for a while. She was so nice, a finer person I have never met.

My aunt was real mean. Sometimes I still wonder how she could have treated me the way she did. I guess, it was a pleasure for her.

* * *

"When did he come in?" I looked up to see Norman. He slipped in quietly, sensing the mood through the sound of our mother's voice. He sat in the large upholstered gray and black tweed high-back rocking chair with the clear plastic cover. All the upholstered furniture in our house was covered in plastic. In the living room, the sofas and matching chairs had custom-made clear plastic slipcovers. I remember the sales man coming to our home with a number of booklets with plastic samples. Some were thick, others thin, in various colors from light pinks, greens, to browns, your choice! Parents in the fifties were making sure that everything lasted, forever.

Sitting on top of folded clothing that made their home there for the past week, Norman's chocolate bowlegs anchored in black and white high-top Converse tennis shoes, were crossed at the ankles.

His handsome face held a serious look. Norman, named after our father, a mirror image of our grandfather, was dependent on me as a little kid, mostly to help settle disputes between him and our older brother, Orlando. He was his own person now, confident, with his own circle of friends, mischievous still, but always kind and generous.

Our mother glanced momentarily at him, but she was not really looking at him, but rather through him. Her thoughts had long since left that room, buried instead in the entangled web of her past, petrified by the memories of the child – no one wanted. That child was screaming and beating on the door of my mother's heart. That child wanted in. My mother would have to make room for her, because that child was not leaving.

I thought about my mother's aunt. My brother's serious face with thick eye brows and curly hair, which I should have – because boys didn't need eyebrows and curly hair - gave me no clues of his thoughts. Frankly, I had no clues of who my mother's aunt was either. She was just someone embodied in meanness, evil like a wicked witch from tales my mother read to us. I remember my mother saying that she was very dark. I imagined her with a muscularly thin body, ectomorphic was the word I learned in fifth grade. My mother never gave me any other details about her, so my imagination ran away with thoughts of her. She looked like a man, sweaty as well, no, more like greasy; and no matter what she wore, she never looked good in her clothes. She never smiled. I was certain of that, because my mother never witnessed it in her presence.

Chapter 2

My mother continued in retrospect, emotionally detached, but physically present.

"I found out that my mother had left me when I was a year old. My grandparents sent her to Cuba, because they did not want her to have anything to do with my father; and funny she never wrote or even bothered to inquire about the child she had left behind. As for my father, I never heard anything of him either. My unmarried granduncle, the one with all those children and different mother's, was good to me. He was like a father, and he liked me a lot."

I wondered why my mother didn't mention the shame the family felt. That is why her mother, Phyllis, was sent away. I never thought that it was my grandmother's choice to leave her baby; but more or less, her duty to respect the dictates of her family. A baby without the bonds of marriage was definitely not supported. It is still not acceptable in my lifetime. I know of girls in my high school and my church who were sent away.

Rightfully *Hers*

My mother told me the story of my grandmother, the girl with the long braid resting on her back. Coming from a proud family, she was sent to a prestigious boarding school on the outskirts of the small parish where they lived, joining other young girls from well-to-do country manor families. She came home, "Knocked up," my mother said bitingly. I thought it odd, strange really, that my mother referred to her beginnings in such common vernacular. My mother never talked that way. But she did that day, and her voice singed in the dusty ashes of her past.

"Yeah," Daphne voiced, slowly emphasizing the words that followed. "They sent her off to that boarding school in a fancy wagon polished from head to foot with the best horses pulling it." She coughed, as if momentarily choked; then continued, "and she came back, knocked up! Swept off her feet by a man in uniform, a constable. Just like that." She spat the words out, then sighed as if exhausted by the recollection.

"Pregnant," she repeated softly in a whispered crackle, while turning her head from side to side. Outwardly, it was clearly a denial. She placed her hands symbolically on her belly. I thought that her insides were churning, not from the anguish of her birth, but from the denial of her mother's love.

Her chest heaved just slightly. She repeated, barely audible with a distant look in her eyes, "Pregnant!" I knew my mother was not talking to me.

I started thinking. 'This was my mother's chance to tell her story, out loud and on paper. What was holding her back?

Didn't she want the world to know?' I thought perhaps that the story was still too painful for my mother to tell; or conceivably, it did not interest my mother, as to why my grandmother became the fragile mother she was. Otherwise, my mother's personal bitterness, her pain, invalidated my grandmother's.

When I tried on another day to probe my mother as to my grandmother's possible pain, I could feel the bitterness raise like bile in my mother's demeanor.

"But Mother," I said, "Grandmother was closed off from everyone and everything she loved. She wasn't even permitted to have anything to do with you."

My mother simply closed her eyes and locked the entry to her heart. There was no justification for what her mother did to her, no ramifications for her actions. That chapter in my mother's life, was systematically sealed. I was a woman before I realized: that chapter in my mother's life was conspicuously opened. The child lost within my mother's person, was angry still.

***

The breeze from the window fan actually felt good, even though my thin arms were feeling a little chilly. My mother paused briefly, possibly reflecting on this omission or quietly dismissing it. There was no rationalization for leaving a child in squalor living conditions, a slave to those around her, and the mother was not dead. My mother continued reading, and just as if she momentarily stumbled, she regained her balance, and her voice sounded happy.

"Well at seven years old, it was time to start school and so I did. The grades were different then. Instead of kindergarten, it was A, then B, then after that it was First through Sixth grades. My first was A, then B, but after staying B for a little while, the teacher thought I was too smart, so I was transferred to the second grade. Well, I was smart. Of course. I was! I caught up with an older cousin. I didn't think she like that, but there was nothing she could do. I was there, and I decided I would stay.

Oh, school days were beautiful. I wished I could do it all over again. Yes, there were days when I was hungry, and moments that I could have died because I didn't get my books on time. Some days, I held on to other children's books, and I could feel them pulling the books away. They didn't want me to touch their books to read from. Still I made good grades. I would always do my best.

In the fourth grade, I passed up another cousin. My grand uncle, the one with those kids and he never married, was real proud of me. He would help me as much as possible with my books and *give me hot buttered buns from his bakery. Even then, I thought that life was wonderful! It was good to be alive."*

There was a sparkling glow in my mother's eyes. That made me feel really good. I watched her sable brown eyes, that were seemingly distant with penetrating pain when she wrote and when she read from her journal. But this day, I could sense happiness in her voice. School had meant everything to her. It was the only leverage that put my mother on equal footing with her cousins and classmates. It supported the person she wanted to be, denied the homeless life she hated and removed her for those precious hours from her sentence of hard labor, because she was a bastard child!

***

"D, I'm home."

I felt a twinge in my stomach. Everything would be different now. My father was home, and that was not something that I liked. The house revolved around him when he was there. He wanted his home, quiet. "Children should be seen, not heard,'" was the proverb from his Jamaican-British upbringing rooted in the core of who he was.

My mother turned quickly to glance at the Seth Thomas bedroom clock. I bet Daphne had a twinge in her stomach too. But she was always prepared to settle the score with my father on her children's behalf. He was home and he was early.

Rightfully *Hers*

My father used this familiar way of addressing my mother, 'D,' short for Daphne. It was an endearment he used only on occasion, but it was a good barometer of his mood, not his usual abrasive manner, walking around the house, checking for things wrong to holler at us kids about.

As a child, I will always remember the fear my father conjured in me. He was not generally physically abusive, but definitely emotional. I remember the one time he struck me, and that incident is permanently cast in my mind.

It was summer break. I was probably in the fourth grade, talking on the phone, a party line, our usual pastime. I was standing in front of the white, built-in corner cabinet gabbing with my girlfriend. I looked absentmindedly into the porcelain plate with the face of Queen Elizabeth, my mother's favorite memento of the 1953 coronation, which my grandmother sent her. The Queen, majestic in her crown jewels, ceremonial ribbons, satin dress, and hair pulled back allowing the crown to be the centerpiece. The Queen's gentle face surrounded by a colorful apple green border had metallic gold threads swirling through it. I looked at this Crown Ducal China plate easily every day, but this day, my father called me. I did not hear him.

He stopped home on his lunch break. A formal and impatient person, my father expected and demanded my immediate attention. I didn't hear him come in the front door, nor did I see him, because my back was turned to him, as I gazed into the plate and talked with my friend. He came from behind and struck me in the left temple, powerfully and swiftly, from a man who trained to be a heavy-weight boxer.

The blow sent me swaying on my feet, falling sideways to the floor. I saw black, as if a lightning bolt zapped the picture from a television set, while it simultaneously removed light from every crevice in the room. Then explosions of colors: red, blood I thought, then orange and yellows, shaped like jarred stars. "Just like in the comic strips," I later told my brothers and mother. I didn't even like those comics, never saw anything funny about being hit over the head with a club. In astonished amazement, I said, "I never thought that stuff was real…. I never thought that you could actually see stars."

As soon as my father left the room, Norman ran to the telephone, to call my mother at work as I struggled with my balance. I tried to hold on to a dining chair, feeling like Helen Keller, blind, isolated, grabbing anything in her path.

I could hear my mother shouting as she entered the house. Norman sat with me at the dining room table. The taste of salt flowed into my mouth and blurred my vision as sweat from my forehead meandered into my eyes. Motionless I was, totally zapped, with Norman trying to comfort me. Orlando was out with his buddies and would be back promptly at 5:00 p.m. to start the family dinner. He was always on time.

"Don't worry Bev," Norman whispered in my ear, his warm breath against my cheek. "Mother is real mad. Daddy's (Daw-di, that's how we pronounced it) not going to get away with what he did to you."

Anger was mounting like a tornado within me, as the winds of my mind flushed through the memories of what happened and why. I was stoic, like a stone with water cascading over my cheek bones, as my breath slowly traveled in and out of my small chest, reminding me that I was very much alive.

My mother walked over to me, turned my sweaty, tear saturated face slowly in her warm, coarse hands. Norman brought ice, a washcloth and remained with me while my parents' argument escalated into my mother screaming. Norman was nervous. I could feel his chest nudging rapidly against my back as he leaned over to help me. I, on the other hand, was just plain mad. Belligerently mad!!! I could have been locked up, put away in juvenile detention until I was 18. I wanted my father dead or just plain gone. My anger's hold on me was so intensifying, my body was shaking.

He didn't like me anyway, I thought. I knew it. This was just another way of his exerting power over me. That five-year separation from his wife and children, somehow, built in him resentment. He probably blamed us for delaying his wife joining him in America. We were just 'mouths' that he was obligated to feed and provide a house for. That was the law. After all, we did not ask to be here.

My mother screamed at my father, "If you ever lay your hands on that child again, I swear, I'll kill you!..."

My father didn't acquiesce, believing instead that I was at fault. I was the one who failed to respond when he spoke to me. But I was relieved to hear my mother's words! He was held accountable!

"You're just a bully. How could you hit a small child like that?" I was thin, had always been thin, but proportioned. I probably weighed about eighty pounds at the time. "You must be sick! You're nothing but a bully," she shouted again.

I could not see my mother's face, nor hear what my father said. I drowned him out completely. I didn't want to hear anything he had to say, anyway. Nothing could validate what this grown man, (I wanted to say, 'This grown ass man, but that would not be polite,') did to me, a child. His hands were larger than my face. My mother was right. He was a bully! If he had done this to me as a child in 2019, he would be arrested; but in the 1950's the proverb was, "Spare the rod, spoil the child."

I sat quietly. My head down, as my breathing labored, and my skin felt clammy, matching the summer afternoon humidity, my thoughts ran away with me. 'Who did he think he was? Why does he think he should have such control over me?...I know I am a child, but I AM HUMAN. I hated him.'

My father, nevertheless, remained alive with a venom that punctuated his heart, alive with hostility he held in his gray eyes, and alive with disdain he edged in his words. But he never touched me again, never hugged me either, but he didn't do that anyway. He never spoke nice to me; but he never hit me again, even when I shouted at him, "I hate you! I hate you!" and ran up the steps to my room, the girl's room. He never followed, demanding that I respect him. On occasions, my mother would make me apologize to him for yelling, "I hate you! I hate you!" I did not want to, but I did it for her to keep peace.

Norman, my father, just sank his muscular body into his large velvet reclining chair, the discarded one he got from the Marriott Hotel when they redecorated - much too big for our space, but no one else could sit in it, and sulked; like I (this little girl) injured him. By the way, my father worked one of his part-time jobs at the Marriott Hotel.

The fear I had of my father was forever present, and never left a conscious level. He had a controlled meanness that was directed at his family or anyone he felt beneath him, our friends and neighbors, or Negro men in America. He firmly believed and was well indoctrinated in the American led propaganda regarding minorities in America. We were undesirable. This posture of course did not include him. He was the brilliant exception.

Cautious of my father's manner: he was capable of inflicting injury just from the weighted, the bullet-piercing tone of his voice, the abruptness and swiftness of his movements personified in the thickness of his muscles, and the piercing penetration of his grayish hazel eyes. Regrettably, kindness was a rare quality in this complex man of many talents and strengths. He was a black man in America, boxed in, not able to live his life to his fullest potential, and in not doing so, he took his frustrations out on his children. We were easy targets!

***

Yes, my father was home. My mother put away her writings for another day and went to place her husband's dinner on the beige brocade table cloth he expected (which I ironed), porcelain plates, sterling silver flatware (that I polished), and his hot cocoa served from a decorative floral teapot with matching porcelain tray, in a teacup and saucer. His children, the last five bathed and dressed in neatly pressed clothes, that I ironed every week, sat passively on the painted forest green swing anchored by chain links from the ceiling of the front porch, playing quietly our invented game, "Choosing Cars."

Chapter 3

Another night slipped in quietly behind the quilted fabric of the sunset. My mother and I bathed the younger kids and put them to bed. She was again ready to read and wanted me to listen, which required no coaxing. Norman strolled in from the hallway clutching a yo-yo. He sat on the corner of our mother's bed, spinning the yo-yo up and down, practicing. He wanted to be as good as Orlando, our older brother, while I rolled my hair on soft pink sponge rollers, and twisted wax paper from 'Wonder Bread' advertising labels. Seemingly relaxed in her night gown and robe, our mother pulled tissue from her robe pocket, completing the ritual. She wiped her brow and continued.

"Then came the day my aunt met a man from another district, and they started courting. In a short time, they were married. Little did I know that my worries had just begun. After the wedding, they decided to move into a half-finished house with three rooms, a kitchen and a bath outdoors. I guess at the time, I was between *nine and eleven years old, and believe it or not, I was the housekeeper.*

Her husband had rented a shoemaker shop from my grand uncle and turned it into a small grocery store. My aunt, being the very, very, lazy type, that was right down her alley. She got to sit down all the time.

I had hoped then that my grand uncle would take me, but he couldn't. In those days, I honestly worked like an old horse."

My mother held on to the word, 'old.' It rolled around on her tongue like she could taste it, and the taste was bitter, like the taste of thick, cod liver oil that my father administered to each of his children on Sunday evenings, lined up from the youngest to the oldest. He used one tablespoon, carefully filling the spoon to the rim each time with the bulging fluid. It wasn't until I was a pre-teen that I was able to escape the "Cod-liberation Ceremony." I told my mother that the oil my father used for all preventative medical issues, made me gag. I felt like I was going to vomit on the spot. My mother excluded me from my father's future line-ups. Orlando was already excluded. I watched Norman in line with our younger siblings as he cut me a look with his eyes, one eyebrow raised high on his head. He used to tell me, "Just do it Bev, so he won't get mad."

I could not! It didn't matter to our father, how I felt; therefore, it didn't matter to me, if he got mad.

***

I had to cook, scrub floors and carry water on my head for about three miles and still get to school on time. It was really rough then. I can't begin to tell you. Only one who passes through it would really understand. I really don't remember how long we lived there. We moved back to her stepmother's home with her younger sister.

A baby was born there to my aunt. My little cousin was so pretty. I loved her! The baby didn't live very long. She died at three months old. The baby just took sick suddenly one Saturday evening, and died Sunday night.

I felt sorry for my aunt then. We all loved the baby so much. Well, it wasn't long before she had another baby, a boy. In spite of the way she treated me, I loved her children dearly and I would do all I could for them. By that time, I became a real slave. I had to get up so early, you couldn't even see your hands before your face. You *had to light a kerosene lamp. That was my usual rounds before and after school every day.*

***

Enraptured by my mother's voice and story, I glanced up to see Orlando, my oldest brother, in the doorway of our mother's room. With the second-floor hallway light out, his yo-yo was glowing neon green in the dark.

I loved to watch him do tricks with his yo-yo, like 'Walk the Dog,' 'Rock the Baby,' and 'Around the World.' He was really good at it, but this night he just stood there, yo-yo, green, in his hand, listening to my mother's voice. He was a good big brother. No one ever messed with me, because other kids yelled, "That's Orlando's sister," and they knew what that meant. 'You better not mess with her!' He was always there to help me.

My mother depended on Orlando to start dinner every day during the week, and he was a good cook. She taught him well, and he understood the blending of ingredients to support mouth-watering dishes. The suggestive smells from his cooking permeated the house, just as my mother's cooking did. He was also a talented artist, would enter contests and get certificates of accomplishments. He was a natural in auto mechanics and could fix any kind of motor.

Orlando was self-taught in a number of areas, including gardening and landscaping. He could fix anything in the house, particularly windows and doors (he and Norman were usually the cause of the breakage) before our parents got home from work. He was quite resourceful. He and my father never got along, - no surprise there.

***

I walked or maybe I should say, I ran home at lunch time. It was rare that there was ever any food prepared for me. I would have to fix it myself. More often than not, I ate crackers and drank sugar and water. I was barefooted, not even shoes for Sunday School, and clothes were very scarce too. My aunt used to fuss so much, constantly reminding me she wasn't my mother and repeatedly stating that I was a burden on her, even though I did all the work.

I knew the taste of sugar and water. My father made my brothers and me drink this mixture one day when we came home for lunch and asked him for lunch money.

My father said, in his distinctive Jamaican accent, "Cha mon, you thinks money grow on trees. There is nothing wrong with sugar and wa'ter. You're just too soft, man!...You think you American, eh? Kiss me neck, man! I said just drink it. You see how strong I am."

He pointed to his big biceps, bulging beneath his shirt. "...I don't want to hear any more about it." But, he did.

As soon as he went upstairs to take his afternoon nap, I called my mother at work to tell her what our father made us have for lunch. It never happened again. I'm sure my father knew that I was the one who made that call.

My mother continued reading as I finished my thoughts about the sugar and water mixture.

Finally, a half-brother of my aunt showed up from St. Thomas. That was a far distance away. He had two grocery stores and wanted her to come and live in St. Thomas to help him. She and her husband decided to leave. Of course, they would not think of leaving the 'little old horse,' me. I was about thirteen in the sixth grade. I was smart. Leaving there meant no more school, and life in general would be hell. I had no choice, after all, no one else had any use for a horse, but her. So, I packed, and we all left. It was a sad parting. I cried, because I was leaving all my friends and relatives, and I really thought that was the end of me.

St. Thomas was nice. The people were O.K. I didn't care too much, because I really missed home. The work seemed harder, because there were two babies and she was expecting another one. I didn't *go to school any more, which really depressed me. Everything was harder.*

Disappointment settled comfortably in my mother's voice. Everything was seemingly different now. School meant so much to her. It placed her in the same shoes as her cousins and classmates. Oddly, their families never gave my mother shoes, not even old ones, or a dress. Maybe, her aunt would not accept them, especially when she could afford to give my mother those things; but didn't want her to have them. Her children wore shoes and clothing purchased at stores.

I knew, however, that school was important to my mother and my grandmother, Phyllis. In her letters to me she always said, "Stay in school....I am so proud of the grades you are making...." My mother sat with me at the dining table as I did my homework. Ready to answer questions. As I got older and the questions were more complex, she would turn the questions around. "How would you answer that question? Why do you think that would work?" When we worked on math problems, my mother's system of getting the answer was different from the way I was taught. But she got the right answer! In school, if I tried to use my mother's system, my teachers would say, 'That's wrong. You can't do it that way.' I was an adult when I realized that there were multiple ways of working mathematical problems.

***

Again, my mother appeared as a child in my mind. Lonely and desperate. Seemingly always edged out at the tape by another runner who thrust his chest forward, knowing he would win, because he was given a head start on the race; but my mother was determined to finish.

My aunt took over her brother's grocery store and her husband opened his grocery store in a little town called Seaport. It was about four or five miles from where we lived. And do you know that I had to take his lunch every day, barefooted and all!

One day before I left home, I found my father's address hidden among my aunt's personal papers and had written to him unknown to my aunt. I told him how badly I was being treated and he sent me some money. I wondered why they never told me who he was, as if I had no right to know. He sent some money, also clothes which I never wore. They were too small.

Even though my aunt got the money, she 'tore my hide' for writing to him behind her back. I didn't care though. I got some things off my chest! A few months after we moved to St. Thomas, I wrote my dad again asking for some aid again, because I was actually naked. I didn't even have a rubber sole shoes for my poor feet. My dad sent some more money. My aunt gave me part of the money to buy a dress in Seaport and crepe sole shoes. I mean gym shoes.

I am looking now at the material I bought.

It had a white background with little pink stripes and a touch of green. I thought it was real pretty. I came home with the fabric for a new dress, all happy. Overwhelmed really! I would have a new dress and it would be pretty. It had been so long since I had worn something like that. But did you know, my aunt 'pitch a fork.'

Yes, I see that fabric too. A soft cotton with a gentle luster, folded like a flag. When placed in the hands of that neglected child by the proprietor, the fabric came to life. The little stripes now pulsating, breathing air into the lungs of the child no one wanted. My mother was bestowed with honor, so rightfully hers. My mother felt deserving. Afterall, she just wanted to look and feel like other children; her little cousins, for example, wearing handsome and pretty garments that her mean aunt bought for them. They even wore shoes when they played.

She said I should have bought some blue chambray, something more practical. That really hurt my feelings, because I had a blue chambray that was 'going down the hill.' It was so big on me. It fit like a huge night gown. I used to tie a string around my waist, so it wouldn't look too bad. I used to go to the river, washed it in my slip, dry it, then put it back on after it dried, and then went home.

Don't feel sorry for me, but I did not change clothes like other children. I rarely ever had more than two, one on my back and one in the tub.

When my mother told me her story of the two dresses, she explained that they weren't really clothing; not like what you would buy in a store, or what a seamstress would make for you. They were gunny sacks, used for hauling yams and potatoes sold in her aunt's grocery store. I wondered why she didn't say that in her writings. Why didn't she say what they really were? Was it embarrassment or shame that snatched that truth from the paper?

The woman sitting before me was one of the best dressed women I knew. My mother always wore beautiful clothes and lovely undergarments. At church, she was the center of attention. People made a big fuss over the garments she wore, and she had a closet full. They were quality clothes, completely lined, void of raw edges with reinforced stitches, pinking shears used under doubled linings and full hems. They

Rightfully *Hers*

were purchased in expensive department stores, bought at the sale price.

I spent a lifetime in stores shopping with my mother. It was a passion she just could not fulfill. Every time the child within her hurt, my mother went shopping. She had accounts at all the major department stores, and she paid every single bill each week from her meager earnings first as a hospital cafeteria worker, then as a housekeeper in a mansion; and she saw to it that every one of her six children looked good too. We would not be reminders of that child in the gunny sack. On Saturday mornings, once our chores were finished (which my father inspected), we went shopping.

Actually, the thought of going shopping, conjured up in me, eating. My mother loved to shop for clothes, furniture, etc. Her children loved the eating! At the end of our shopping day, our mother always took us to the popcorn store, where we could select popcorn in all kinds of flavors. The clerk placed our balls in wax paper sacks, where we ate them on the bus or when we got home. Usually, it was when we got home, because we had too many packages in our hands. Yummy!

Norman said, "What are you going to eat, Beverley? I know what I'm having."

My stomach started churning. But the thought of going to the Grant store food counter was always appealing to me, and my mother allowed us to select whatever we wanted from the limited lunch menu.

"I think that I'll have Fried Chicken," I said. "It's the best."

Norman smiled, "Yep, it's real good, but first, I'm having my favorite, Root Beer Float. Hires (the manufacturer)is calling me, sis." Norman grinned brightly, placing his hands on his hips, in a western cowboy stance. There was always a Hires Root Beer sign at the luncheonette, with a picture of the ice cream float. It looked delicious!

"You having your favorite, Bev," asked Norman?

"Yeah, a strawberry malt sounds really good to me."

I knew I couldn't eat all that chicken and a malt, but I knew my Mother would help me eat it, because the chicken came with fries, and Norman would have some too. Norman loved fries.

At Grants, we could actually eat at their luncheonette counter, a Formica top with silver metal wrapped around the edges and round circular vinyl fabric seats attached to silver pole bases. The waitress waited on us right away, if white people were not there. It was a small area, so our mother saw to it that her children were seated and fed, then paid our bill, while she walked the nearby aisle for merchandise. If we went to Woolworth's, we could shop there, but we were not allowed to eat there, because of our color.

Once a year, usually at the end of October or the beginning of November, the Amish people came to town and went shopping too. I was really fascinated by these people. Horse and buggies lined the blocks where few stores were located, to avoid upsetting the horses when cars went by. The policemen redirected traffic away from the horses.

All the boys wore the same clothes, as did all the girls. Girls wore mid leg dresses, we called tea length, usually a plaid pattern with sleeves. A long navy blue or brown cotton bibbed apron was worn over the dress. They all wore the same black leather laced top shoes to almost their knees, and bonnets covering their hair. They reminded me of watching pioneer movies. The women wore the same shoes, but solid colored dresses in brown or dark blue and a bonnet.

Men in long beards, wearing tall hats like President Lincoln, long sleeved solid cotton shirts and black leather boots just below their calves, jotted across the street.

"Boy, this is neat," Norman said, as we stood there with our mother. She held our hands. I think she was nervous about the horses. Orlando had more freedom, so he was constantly moving around, finding interesting things for us to look at. But the day the Amish came to downtown Indianapolis, they were the only people we were interested in.

I agreed with Norm. The Amish were really neat and could not take my eyes off them. The girls stayed together, as they crisscrossed the street in multiple rolls, paying no attention to the lights. We called that Jaywalking. The police wrote tickets for this, but there were just too many Amish; and they had their own rules. Paid no attention to our rules! The streets were really crowded with on-lookers like me and my family on the sidewalks in front of the stores, gazing at our visitors. I loved those days. I wished they came more often. It was like looking at our world a hundred years ago through an hourglass.

By the time we got home, with all those bags, my father would be at work. So, he never really knew how much shopping we actually did. By the time he got home, all the purchases were put away.

But my father always seemed delighted when he saw how nice she and the children looked on Sundays going to church. We certainly presented the image he wanted for his family, 'successful'.

Shopping with Daphne required patience, because it was never just the price, it was always the quality. And did she love shoes, shoes of every color, for any occasion, just for that barefoot child.

Shoe boxes were stacked in one corner of my mother's bedroom next to the closet, midway to the ceiling, others under the bed and in the closet. Each pair stored in the original box that it was purchased in.

Every outfit she had was completely accessorized – numerous earrings, necklaces, and scarves, as well as nylon and silk stockings, with reinforced toes and heels, in all colors. The child who wore a string around her waist, owned countless belts made of different fabrics, textures and colors, as well as wool coats, raincoats, furs (minks), mutton lamb, and fox tails with their little heads and black beady eyes dangling over her shoulders, which was the style. I don't remember my mother having cashmere coats, but my father had two handsome ones, black and camel color.

***

Rightfully *Hers*

As I sat on the corner of my mother's bed, she continued to read.

Yet I don't think that I ever lost my smile; and by then I could really talk to my God. My aunt's stepmother had taught me that. She always said, 'You're not too young to pray and you can talk to God just like you sit here and talk to me.' Believe me, I really did! At times, it seemed he didn't hear me, but I kept on telling him my troubles anyway.

As her aunt's stepmother taught Daphne to pray, my mother taught us to pray as well. "Now I lay me down to sleep. I pray the Lord, my soul to keep. If I should die before I wake, I pray the Lord, my soul to take." I was always a little uncomfortable with the last line. I didn't really want anyone to take my soul; but our mother taught us this, so I thought it must be okay. Then our prayers were followed by a litany of "God Bless Mother, Daddy (I didn't really want to say that either)...."

When we said grace at the dinner table, Orlando spoke first, "God is great, and God is good." Then Norman, "And we thank him for our food." Beverley, "By his hands, we are fed." Then all three of us recited, "Give us Lord, our daily bread." With the addition of our siblings born in America, our parts were reduced, so each child had a phrase in the blessing as it rotated around the table.

***

The next day's reading required coaxing, not from the listeners, but from the reader. My mother was already in tears with dry heaves mounting in her chest in large swells, and she hadn't even started reading yet.

"Do you want me to read it for you, Mother," I offered?

"I'll do it," retorted Norman. "You can just relax and take it easy, Mother."

We waited. Then our mother shook her head from side to side, making it clear that she intended to continue in her usual manner. So again, we children just waited for her as our expectations grew, wondering, 'What could it be?' My heart was throbbing in my chest.

Like a car running out of gas, my mother restarted her engine. She repeated the sentence from the night before. I suppose she thought that her children had forgotten where she left off.

"At times, it seemed that he didn't hear me, but I kept on telling him my troubles anyway."

My mother took a deep breath, pulled Kleenex from her pocket, and the ritual was again completed. However, the pain that followed wrecked her soul while diminishing her strength, as her children inspected the outward injury of the woman sitting before them; inwardly we were lost, as was she, in the thick, rugged jungles of our mother's past.

I even in those early days prayed to die. Sometimes, I lost faith, because I would sit and cry.

I mean really cry, because life didn't seem worthwhile to live. I couldn't understand why mine was the way it was. I couldn't understand why I had to hide and watch other children go to Sunday School. I looked so bad; I couldn't let them see me looking at them. So, I would hide and watch them with their parents, wearing pretty little dresses. It seems now like just a dream; but it's the truth that I am writing on this paper, so I use black ink.

Amid the gigantic Banana Plants with fruit in abundance, split leaf Philodendrons, ferns, palm trees of all varieties, pruned only by nature as the child within its foliage, Daphne stood. In the dark crevice of her pain, she was alone as was expected, isolated as predetermined. Daphne hid her nakedness as she watched the parade of children, girls particularly in pretty dresses, with families on their way to church.

As the church bells in the distance rang, Daphne felt the vibration through her bare, crusted soles. She could literally taste the sorree, mangoes and bananas on the breeze, whipping through the moist air; but she wasn't hungry for food – only for the life other children lived. Every week, the minute her aunt and family pulled off in their small horse-drawn buggy, Daphne, practically naked, ran across the road to this haven. Her own natural steeple waited, the plants towering above her, glowing within God's paradise. There Daphne witnessed life as she knew it could be.

After the children passed, the reverberating quietness provided Daphne time to think, away from her mean aunt who constantly reminded her that she was a burden and a "bastard child." Each week, she turned quickly from her little cousin, who repeatedly asked his mother, "Why Daph no go?"

Her aunt waved her hand in annoyance, then ushered her son out the door. Daphne stood, eyes transfixed on the floor, knowing that this was her time to commune with God. She would not go, nor would she ever go to church with this family. She was not a member of their family, she was help. More accurately, she was a slave, not deserving of love and attention.

Daphne looked for God through the fleshy tree branches, where sweltering heat and light could barely penetrate. Time stood still embracing the child whose heart was pierced, penetrated by the loss of her mother's love. The tears cascading over the child's soft, golden image were, ironically, the only tangible evidence of her injury.

I wanted to touch her, to pull her into the brilliant sunlight, to smile and laugh with her; to turn her around, hand-in-hand, while playing 'Ring around the Rosie,' and watch the powerless, neglected, ragdoll transform into a beautiful African princess. My mother emotionally read on.

I couldn't understand how a mother could have a child, her own child, and not even bother to find out if it is alive or dead, and up to this very minute. I am now a mother of seven. I lost my first baby girl. Next January 18, I will be forty years old, but I am still wondering why my own mother turned her back on me. I will never stop wondering why.

My mother underlined places in her writings when she was angry and could not understand why these things were happening to her: "So I use Black Ink;" "I will never stop wondering why." This child was neglected with no avenue for support, nowhere to go, who would want her? After all, her grandfather selected this woman for her care. And this woman deeply resented this child's involvement in her life for any reason. She obeyed the grandfather, took the child; but held the posture that since the child's mother was not dead, this responsibility should not have fallen to her. Hatred built up within her for this intrusion into her life. So, Daphne had no place for refuge, but the natural protective vegetation that God provided.

***

Now, I know you are wondering what happened to my pretty dress fabric? My aunt gave it to a woman across the street from her shop who made it into a dress. I was very pleased even though I knew it would not last too long, not when you have to wash it often.; but it was wonderful to wear something that was made right and looked nice.

***

The owner for the place we lived in was real nice. We got along fine, but on Fridays when I had to go with them about twelve miles out of town and carry a big basket of yams on my head, I wished many a day, I didn't know them. My aunt didn't care, because she was getting the food free.

I could feel the weight of the yams in a basket on my mother's small head and could sense her anger in having to carry these vegetables for miles. How could they do that to a little girl, just because they could? So, they got free food and free transport, that being my mother. I am sure, her aunt sold the yams in her little grocery store. So, her aunt was very happy!

Chapter 4

Well out of all evil came some good. My uncle wrote to tell me my mother was in Kingston, the Capital of Jamaica, and sent me her address, saying I must write to her. I was so happy just to know that I would have a mother, was something to really shout about. I wrote my mother and she answered quicker than I expected. After a few letters, I was able to tell her a little more each time. The most exciting thing in one letter was I would be getting some new clothes. I was really happy about that. I looked forward to seeing that package.

   At last it came, and believe me, they were the prettiest clothes, I had seen, but they couldn't fit, not one. They were all too small. I sent back to tell her, and even then, I was happy knowing they were mine."

I had a hard time with the fact that each time a gift of clothing came for my mother, it was too small. This happened first with her father. I could understand why my grandfather would not have knowledge of children's clothing. But when the same thing happened from my grandmother, I could not accept that. My grandmother was a seamstress after all. She understood measurements and did this for a living, every day, in Cuba. She knew what it took to make a good fit. But Phyllis must have lived in a dream world. Imagined my mother only as she pictured her in her mind, a little girl, without height and girth. How could she? A beautiful dress was more important to my grandmother, than the simple fact that the dress could not fit this child. Yet when I looked at my mother, there was no evidence of loss in her eyes, only gain. The knowledge that the clothes were meant for her, sustained her. It was all she needed.

Perhaps some other child would have cried, but I didn't as a matter of fact. I didn't cry much. I just knew somehow, somewhere, the Lord would take care of everything; and then life went on and on, but I was determined not to lose contact with my mother. The most wonderful news came in one of her letters. She was coming up to see me. My aunt was given the news, and in her heart, she had to make some changes. She did. I got one more dress, and we all looked forward to seeing her.

52

The day finally came, and I think it was about 4 p.m. It was a surprise and a big one. Only one thing, hearing people talk of her and being a child, the imagination I built inside of me — what she was like, funny it wasn't like her. But I was very glad to see her, and right that very moment, I began to wonder how it would be to live with a real mother. Well she stayed two weeks and those two weeks were the most wonderful I had ever seen or enjoyed. Things were so wonderful, but my aunt was just trying to show her that I was well taken care of, and I didn't have to work hard, which I really didn't during her stay. It looked completely so.

I told her everything though, that what she was seeing was only a front. During her stay, I really wondered what she really thought of me. One thing that really puzzled her was the way I had grown. She was looking for a smaller child. Oh, I just wished I could see and hear what her heart was saying about me. Maybe I could have been mistaken, but somehow, I thought she didn't care too much, and after all, who could blame *her. I don't think she wanted to be bothered anyway with children.*

What a burden for a child to carry! Here my mother was concerned that her mother may not want her. I looked into Norman's eyes. He didn't say anything. He just sat there quietly, wondering as I did, whether our mother would have chosen us, an uncomfortable thought. I was glad that I wasn't victimized by such reflections.

I bet I knew what my grandmother, Phyllis, was really thinking. 'Ma Lord, what me gonna' do with this wo-man. She no child. How me get so confused? Me thought me coming to visit a child, and me find a little woman here. My God, where did the years go? How come she look only like the father? Where me is in her?'

'I don't see me in this child a'tall. She yella', with freckles and red hair. Just like her father! Me don't think me can do this. I know the child feels she mistreated, but me thinks she be better off here. At least the children take to her.'

Then my grandmother, Phyllis, probably took a deep breath, fighting off the panic and tears she felt coming. 'Me must handle meself properly. This woman child will neva' know what me really thinking. Yes, Lordy! Me can do it. Yes, me can do it.'

Well after two wonderful weeks, she was off back to Kingston, I was left behind to return to the backbreaking work — washing, ironing, cooking, carrying water, and oh it's too much to mention. One thing though, I had some hope. My mother promised me she would send for me as soon as she got back and was settled. That was a lot to look forward to.

Life with my aunt as I see it now was horrible, and it makes me wonder now and more every day — <u>why</u> any woman who is a mother also would treat another woman's child the way they treated me. If I even asked a question, I never got an answer. In other words, I was just some kind of an animal, but life went on day after day. I was sure some way I could get out of it.

In the silence that followed, my mother's words echoed in my mind, "I was just some kind of animal...." She spoke those words without resolve or even malice. She was debased to mere subsistence. Yet, I was puzzled by her voice. It was flat, without the rage I expected. From my school readings, I recognized that many slaves were treated like this: Imprisoned in silence. My mother was property, nothing more, everything less than! But like a thin blade of grass pushing its way through a minuscule opening in a concrete walkway, I found in my mother's words that hope was still alive in that emotionally shackled child.

***

In a reflex action, I fingered the gold birdcage-like charm that held a mustard seed around my neck. My mother bought the necklace for me and told me that the mustard seed was a symbol of hope. Dangling on threadlike gold links, the charm felt warm and smooth between my fingers.

The Sunday she gave this gift to me, I was changing clothes after church. My mother walked in. "I want you to have this," my mother said pensively, with no other introduction. "It's for you."

I initially saw Mother in my mirror, then turned on the vanity stool to face her. She held a small blue velvet box in her hand.

"You are my oldest daughter, and you are developing into quite a young lady. I'm real proud of you."

Moisture glistened on my mother's freckled skin, and her eyes were magnified through tears barely on the surface. It was as if I was looking at pebbles just beneath cool waters, magnified and polished. My upstairs bedroom, on the other hand, was hot and humid.

"I hope you have rich soil. Nothing like my rough life! God, I wouldn't want any of my children to struggle like I did. No mother to help me, no dad! No one ever wanted me, that's why I work so hard for you children."

I looked into her eyes. They were reflective again as the mention of her past weighted her down. She returned to me, now standing before her, in nylon panties and a soft padded bra. Through the realization of what the mustard seed charm symbolized, my mother continued her thoughts.

"But, you can make it Babs." On occasion, my mother called me 'Babs.' It was not a nick name. Norman sometimes called me 'Bevs'.

Yet this day, I felt like I was going through a special rite of passage. From childhood to womanhood with the full knowledge that faith, hope and charity would somehow sustain me. My mother's focus was now 'Hope.' Charity and faith, she had already given me.

In the background, the window fan churned tirelessly. I was hoping that I could get dressed, before my father came in from church to tell me to turn the fan off. However, if my mother was in my room, he would not say anything. While the fan hummed quietly, it provided a monotone milieu, as my mother opened the box while saying, "But you can make it." She put the dark blue velvet box down on the dresser, then connected the closure around my slim neck and fastened it.

"Just like this mustard seed. The soil won't matter, because there is hope within that seed. It can sink its roots into the toughest soil and grab hold on life. If you have hope, just the size of this mustard seed! That is all you'll need. God will do the rest!"

I had misgivings about the financial sacrifice my mother made to give me this gift; but I didn't mention it. It was a gift after all. She was a housekeeper in a mansion where she took care of five children. She didn't have money just lying around.

I cherished, however, that moment and gift. In my mother's embrace, I knew that hope derives its strength from the heart of the soul that gives.

Mother and I still corresponded, and she would send me little pocket money by the bus driver. Well, I guess her visit changed me somehow. I was determined to leave, and as the days passed on, I was nearer that goal.

One Monday morning as usual, I got up for breakfast, got the babies things and dirty clothes together. My aunt washed the baby's things, while I walked about five miles to Seaforth to take her husband's lunch. It was after midday when I got back, picked up my clothes and headed for the river to wash. It was after 5 P.M. when I got back. In the kitchen I had to get out all over the place to find wood for the fire and then our dinner was on. I cooked and she shared as usual, but during the rush, I forgot to take the baby's diapers and clothes off the line. When her husband came in, I guess after 8 P.M. He saw the clothes on the line and wanted to know what they were still doing on the line. I started to explain what my chores were for the day, and that I had forgotten them. Well,

I guess as a slave, I didn't have any right to talk back to my Boss. So, he came at me and hit me.

I must have said everything and told him off, in and out. He picked up a piece of board and hit me again. I catch it with my hand and got a cut, also I had scratches on my face and neck. I just hollered. I guess you could hear me blocks away; but that was it, when he raised his hand to strike me. That was his mistake. Right now, I am writing and still thinking of some of the things I didn't tell him that I should have; but of course, I am so close to forty years old. I have a lot more experience and could have handled him well.

I was no longer comfortable with my intrusion into my mother's life, by invitation. So, I glazed absentmindedly through her bedroom window. Night brought on its own seclusion and secret changes. I saw the majestic Maple tree from the front yard in the moonlight and heard the strangely familiar, metallic voice of the 17-year locust. That's what us kids called them; but I learned later that they were actually cicadas. In the mornings, I would see a shiny-golden, pastry-thin shell, anchored to the bark of the Maple tree, with a slit down its back, the cicada having escaped its enclosure.

Norman and Orlando carefully pulled the empty crusts from the bark. They were so fragile, they could easily be destroyed;

but of course, there were plenty insects. I saw the casings all the time.

Orlando pretending that he was going to put the papery shell on me, ran towards me yelling, "Bevs, I got something for you."

I stood my ground, because I knew he would not put that insect shell on me.

Norman, running behind him with sturdy bowlegs said, "I got something too, Bev!"

With Norman, I couldn't be sure, but I knew it was not likely that he would throw the shell on me; but I never knew. Instead, he brought the sugar like enclosure over for me to examine. I picked up a twig, slowly and carefully, pushing the crustacean over, observing all the intricate parts. I never used my hands to pick up the nasty remains. Dried, crispy bodily fluids of some sort, Yuck!

The irascible, thick, iridescent black and green insect was ready to meet its challenges in the new world.

This insect is not one to reckon with. It spends about 13-17 years burrowing underground as larva, before surfacing. It doesn't have long to live once it emerges.

My mother thought she didn't have long to live either. But like the cicada, I knew my mother was determined to surface, and find the sunshine in her life as well.

So that night, I sat down to write my mother, and told her all that had happened. I said in my letter that I was coming home to her and wanted money for my fare. The following Thursday, the money came, also a letter telling me how to come there. I was so happy when my aunt's husband brought the letter and money, threw it down on the table, when I set his dinner down. It was a wonderful moment. Then he said to my aunt, 'The gal's mother sent for her.'

I guess I came in through the door, as he handed her my letter, and threw money down, before she could say a word. She read it. I guess they talked about it. I didn't have time to listen, because I had to wash dishes, and my only concern was to LEAVE.

I decided that I would not leave in a hurry, but that I would answer my mother, telling her to look for me the following week, because I wanted to do right in spite of everything. Those last days were days I will remember for the rest of my life. I was happy, carefree, nothing mattered. I cleaned the kitchen and the house as I had never done *before, and only one thing in those last days – Daphne didn't take any orders and didn't give any. I know that my aunt could have died, but it was only getting later all the time.*

This is the first time I had heard my mother use her name, Daphne, in her writings. It was carefully calculated. It was the first time, she felt that she was in a position of power, her first taste of freedom, and she liked that acrid taste. It was strangely satisfying. My mother was not alone.

A couple of nights, before I left, her husband came in to argue. He wanted to know since the gal was leaving, what was my aunt going to do? That was the first time I heard her say, she would miss me, and that I had been good help to her. He said, 'She hasn't been able to catch any man here, so she is going in town where she can catch them as she likes.'

Those words left my mother's mouth with the same anger they conjured up in her a lifetime ago. The hostility and loathing she felt for her uncle, although she never called him 'uncle' in her writings, were still alive in the woman reading before me. I was angry too, that this man would beat up a child, using a board from a fence. What kind of people were these? He, just like her aunt, denied my mother's worth, then he had the gall to imply that my mother was only interested in men. She was only a little girl. I'm pretty sure that children didn't marry at that age in the Jamaican culture, like arranged marriages in Asian cultures; so, it appeared to me that he was just being mean. I hated him too.

Well that was one question I wanted to answer for Berron Russell; and I didn't get to give it to him. About two or three years after, he died like a dog and now as a full-grown woman, it would have been a great pleasure to answer him. So, let bygones be bygones.

Who was Berron Russell? My mother never used his name before. Probably because, he was the one in the back, hiding in the shadows. The one from the phrase, 'in the corner, in the back, in the dark.' One of those people who see abuse and misuse, but never have the guts to stand up to it. He was probably glad that it was not him that his mean wife turned her anger on. Maybe he felt that my mother got just what she deserved. Afterall, Daphne was not his wife's child. She was the bastard child of that uppity Phyllis living in Cuba, who didn't give a damn about the child she spurned. So why should he?

The tragedy in what he willingly allowed was that he participated in the demise of my mother. He knew he was sacrificing Daphne for his own children. He saw no value in Daphne other than as an animal. An animal should be grateful to have food, water, shelter. It needed nothing else. So, he figured that Daphne needed nothing else. Daily, he worked for his own son and daughter, making sure that they had what they needed, and what he wanted them to have. Daphne was not his obligation.

As Berron Russell goes into obscurity, there will be a number of Berrons to take his place.

***

The following Friday, I had everything of mine packed. By four o'clock, I was ready to leave; but it wasn't a happy parting. He wasn't home and my aunt had two babies which I loved dearly, and it broke my heart to leave them. I would lie awake at night during those last few days and wondered what would become of the children, how I would miss them and they me.

But I had to leave. I couldn't let the children stop me. It was their parent's problem, not mine. I had to get out!

When the truck came by, the young man named Eric, called out asking if I was ready. I said, 'Yes.' Then I showed him my things and went to the grocery store to say good-bye to my aunt.

I could have cried. She had one baby standing by her side and one in her arms. The one in her arms stretch for me to take her. I couldn't. It was most touching, because though I was only fourteen years old, I was more of a mother to these children than my aunt was.

I thought about my mother. The child who had no mother, was an excellent, caring mother. The child who had no books was an engaging student. The child with no shoes was a spirited runner, and the child with no clothes, was showered in God's loveliness.

When I turned to go, she said without any kindness, 'Here is a shilling. Bye.'

I took it and even now I wonder why I did take it. That was my end with her, her husband and her children. I never wrote to her, didn't intend to. I wanted no more of her, 'NO MATTER WHAT!'

Chapter 5

My trip to Kingston, Jamaica was pleasant at least. I was sure life would be different. I had hope and faith for a different life. The one behind was hard, rough, rugged, not the kind any young girl with ambition would appreciate. I would say that we reached Kingston after midnight, and my mother was there to meet me. I went home with her to 99 Orange Street.

There I was to begin my new life, meet new faces, and on a whole try a new start. My thoughts and intentions were to finish high school, which was shattered when my Mother told me that she could not afford to send me. Well, it didn't take long for me to find out that with mother, life was not going to be a bed of roses, but I was determined to try my best to make a go of it. I started out by going to find a job which wasn't easy, because I was young and should be going to school. Now no one to look to, so I took to the streets.

***

I could hear my grandmother talking to her herself, agitated, like my mother shared with me, 'Lordy, Lordy, how me gonna make it with this woman child. She nothing but trouble. Me would send her to school, but for what happenchance? Girl children not worth it. You hear me Lord! Me know this. Not worth it! Let her get a job. Get her off me hands.' Phyllis then slapped her palms together, symbolizing her withdrawal from her daughter's life.

Phyllis could feel the anger mounting inside, 'Why me Lord, why me? Girl children nothing, but shit....nothing but Shit. Me sorry fa saying that, Lord! But tis true, simple truth,' she confirmed. Then tears flooded the threshold of her continence.

***

I must find a job. I went to many places where they just looked at me, and said, 'we can't use you.' I ended up at a perfume factory, "Solomon Khris Krush Factory." The manager was a blind man. His name was Izzet Solomon. He told me to come back next week. I went there for two weeks, just about every day. Then finally his secretary said, 'Mr. Solomon, the little girl is here again.'

He said, 'Bring her to me.' He felt my arms, my height. Then he asked how old I was and why I wasn't in school?

I told him I had to have a job, then I could go to night school. He called down the head of the upstairs department and her name was Mrs. Howell. He said, 'I have a little girl here you may be able to use for any little thing.' So finally, I was hired and that was the beginning of a new life.

Working was wonderful in every way. I was helping myself and looking forward to high school, music lessons. More than all, I was getting away from the people who didn't seem to want me around. It seemed that I was nothing else but trouble to the people who were closest to me, and that's a very sad situation to live with. There were times I wondered if I had done the right thing leaving my aunt, because there was lot of joy with her children.

My mother blinked her eyes, and her face darkened. I imagined a veil of rejection covering the face of the child no one wanted. I tried to look through the netting shading my mother's eyes; but they revealed nothing. Each weave neatly meshed in years of isolation and silent suffering camouflaged behind the see-through veil wall. My mother blinked her eyes again as if to hide any documents of despair remaining.

At least, the people I worked with were all very nice to me. I guess because I was so young. The owner, Mr. Solomon, always asked about that little girl. Sometimes, I wanted to tell him I had a name, DAPHNE, but then it really didn't matter. I had a job and I was so thankful to God things were really changing.

***

After the death of her grandmother and great grandmother, Grandam, my mother was alone and knew only cruelty from her aunt. She did, however, know love from Uncle Harold and her little cousins.

It took fourteen years for my mother's dream to actually be fulfilled. Now, she was like the other children she watched from the side of the road. She had a mother. She was so happy. I could feel her heart beating profusely in her chest. Her new life would start now.

Regrettably, she quickly learned from her own mother, "Girl children ain't nothing but shit!" She was not wanted by my grandmother, Phyllis, either. Daphne was a daily reminder in my grandmother's mind of what she lost. That is why she didn't come to get her. Phyllis blamed her daughter for ruining her life. She was angry still. It certainly did not help that Daphne looked like her father. How is it that your own mother does not want you? I was plagued by such knowledge. It's just not right!

Her mother believed that sending girl children to school was a waste of money. Now, where did she get that from? Mr. Solomon, who could not see my mother's eyes, had no idea what she looked like, because he was blind, but he could see into her heart. He sensed from this child determination to make her own life better, she would succeed.

***

Mother was still unmarried, but there was always a man around. And they always seemed to be struggling. So, most of the time, my money went to help pay rent and other bills. Another thing I found out quickly was that Mother did not get along with other folks who lived around.

In her writings, Daphne wrote, "Mother did not get along with other people." But her words to her children, "My mother despised the people we lived around, and cursed them, 'fuckin' bastards…You betta' keep out of me fuckin' business, ya hear!' every chance she got…. It was so embarrassing."

I learned early that the cultured girl, my grandmother, who was sent to the best boarding schools, had everything that the girl of the manor should have, had acquired a commoner's street savvy that she hurled like an angry child throwing rocks at anyone who did not bend to her wishes.

She always seemed so unhappy. We did not get along as a real mother and daughter does. There was that gap between us that couldn't be filled; but funny, everyone seemed to love me. I guess they felt pity, because Mother and I were so different.

I realized that my mother and I were different as well. Even though we both had freckles, we didn't look alike.

I looked more like my father and was the splitting image of his younger sister Lolita. This was perplexing for him at times. My father often called me 'Lolita,' but I would not answer. In fact, I refused to answer. My father didn't respect me anyway.

He shouted angrily, "You know I'm talkin' to you!"

Silence was my only response, which made my father angrier. Neighbors got my aunt and me confused as well. I was fifteen and my aunt, who was visiting, was about forty-five, that's how much we looked alike.

But with my mother, our personalities were different, yet complimentary. We always got along fine, not because we were alike. It was because my mother embraced our differences, making me feel special. There was never any doubt about the love between us, shared openly and privately. But I sensed the longing in my mother's voice. It is important to have a mother to love and to be loved by. It is the basic need of all children, and my mother was no exception.

***

Believe me, it was easy at the time to smile and really wonder, it there was a mistake somewhere. One thing for sure, she had never wanted a child. She just couldn't hide it. Then one day she told me how much I had messed up her life. There were even times when she would introduce me as her sister. Mother sewed for a living, a seamstress.

***

Again, my mother wrote neatly in her writings, "She told me how much I had messed up her life." But her verbal accounts to her children were far more graphic, "Whenever the opportunity presented itself, my mother shouted at me. 'Little Red Bastard! You fucked up my life!...Girl children ain't worth wastin' money on!...' She cried as she said these things. Phyllis was always crying."

My grandmother, Phyllis, was always two distinctly different women in my mind. First, the common street person, I never met; but my mother knew that person well; and secondly, the cultured lady I became acquainted with through her letters and gifts.

The woman my mother told me about, who conjured up such painful longings in the heart of a child, now woman, was not the woman I met at age thirteen and was re-acquainted with. I met the tall, regal, formal woman from her many conventional letters, which were punctuated properly, like the writings of an English teacher. She said things like, "It's of no consequence! Too late to examine now....Do not trouble yourself with such matters...." She was full of life, like the skirt she sent me for my tenth Birthday.

Yes, she sent lovely gifts: clothes, table linens, blackened rum soaked cakes, bottled hot peppers which made your eyes water when you opened them, fresh mint-smelling bay leaf rubbing alcohol, odd looking dried cocoa directly from the plant, poignant ginger root, a 150 proof Jamaican rum, that My mother would take a spoonful and add to the family Kool-Aid at Sunday dinners, and of course, my favorite, Tamerin Balls. My brothers and I would get two to three balls, the size of a cotton ball, every two to three days, until they were gone.

My favorite gift from my grandmother was the beautiful hand-painted canvas skirt she sent for my tenth Birthday. The colors were spectacular, riding above the beige canvas medium. It was marvelous, with tropical birds flying, red and yellow hibiscus, you could figuratively lift from the cloth. The skirt was a history lesson with every item marked and identified in black acrylic paint lettering. I turned my body around and around, watching the skirt flare out about my thin body. The skirt came to life, before my eyes. I felt like I was right there in Jamaica, running through the countryside, feeling the moist grasses between the toes of my bare feet, or the chilling waters slapping over my hot body as I followed a guide while navigating massive rocks at the Dunn's River Falls. In its European–like capital Kingston, with thousands of people headed to work, in pristine dress, constables wore formal dress, directing traffic. I was alive in that skirt. My fifth-grade teacher asked me to model that skirt for my classmates. I was the center of attention. I was proud.

These dazzling images on that hand-painted skirt, bonded me to my grandmother as no other visual ever had or ever could. It became the essence of my vibrant grandmother, whom I would love for a lifetime, but was just actually getting to know.

I remember my grandmother taking me to the market in Jamaica at age thirteen. We rode the city bus, with people packed liked sardines in a can; but she stood out, stately, confident, as she navigated the bus ride and stores. She seemed to know everyone, introducing me to many people, "This is my granddaughter, Mistress Beverley, from America…. Good day to you, Sir…." Smiling as I looked into seemingly hundreds of faces who always responded, "Well, how do you do?" whether they were wearing a well-tailored suit or a round neck sweaty sleeveless undershirt, grinning wide, with or without teeth.

***

Yet, now, I was just beginning to realize and understand the depth to which my mother actually loved her mother, my grandmother, Phyllis. From the time I was old enough to understand, my mother never spared me the pain of her mother's cruelty. In her writings, however, she protected Phyllis by discreet omissions. She told me many of the heartfelt conversations she had with her mother. One example was how she had to pay the rent with her paycheck which she mentions, but she does not go on to tell in her writings, how often, she was awakened in the middle of the night to move out. Her recollections were always told to us in details. Maybe, she just did not feel like writing it all down, or possibly those details were just for us.

"Wake up child." Phyllis spoke in a hushed whisper as she shook her daughter's arm. Daphne looked into her mother's narrow face, the room illuminated by the light of the moon, which highlighted Phyllis' aquiline nose like her own.

"Come on child, me no have all night!"

Daphne sat up, momentarily confused while focusing her eyes.

'Granddam,' Daphne initially thought, waking from a pleasant dream. "Granddam?" Daphne said instinctively remembering her sweet great grandmother.

"What wrong with ya' girl?"

"Ya hear me, gal!" The whisper supported her mother's full warm breath with a tinge of garlic, remembering Granddam, which added a sense of urgency.

Daphne, awakened now, looked across the room. Several bags were on the floor of the apartment.

"Where we going?" Daphne asked.

"Don't bother me with ya stupid questions child." She handed Daphne a dress. Daphne began quickly dressing.

Now, feeling she owed her daughter an explanation, she continued. "Me can't stay here. You thinks me would let him harass me so. Me have no intentions of putting up with his fuss…. Him sorely mistaken if him thinks me would stay here. Not even a decent bed," she extended her arms toward the bed. "Me no put up with this mess any longer." Phyllis moved swiftly toward their bags on the floor.

"Him find someone else to put up with this shit!" Her mother made a hissing sound. Daphne knew she was sucking her teeth, which Phyllis often did when angry. Daphne heard her mother arguing with the manager earlier in the evening. Now she made the connections.

In the back of her mind, Daphne knew that her mother had not paid the rent again.

Daphne and Phyllis, packed with bags cramping their hands and fingers quietly left in the middle of the night, like thieves. The manager, soundly asleep in a unit nearby, never heard them exit. This scenario was repeated on a number of other occasions. Always in the night, with Phyllis cursing and blaming the manager beneath her breath, while Daphne wondered what her mother did with the money, she contributed to the rent, from her job at the perfume factory.

She also had a few women friends who were married to Chinese. One especially, I think her name was Era. She had a nice home and children. Her husband had a large grocery store. Mother wanted very much for me to be like Era., but I don't think she was the type to land one of these Chinese. So, she decided to work on me. She always told me; the Chinese man would take better care of me than a black man.

My mother's best friend was Chinese. We called her Aunt Phyllis. She was married to a short black, older man. She was a beautiful woman, with a rounded, flat face and wide cheekbones. She had straight dark brown hair, almost black. Initially her hair was long, but later she cut it into the stylish bob of the 50's. Aunt Phyllis was tall and usually wore pants. She was a 'stay at home' mom – widely accepted in the fifties. My mother was the one who was different – she worked outside of the home. Aunt Phyllis was so nice and pretty. I loved being with them. Seeing the joy in my mother when the two were together was really special. They were always laughing. I sat quietly, listening to their conversation, like a fly on a wall. Aunt Phyllis was truly kind and generous and could really cook. My mother loved for her to make fresh baked rolls, which were so tender, they formed delicate webs on your fingertips, and melted in your mouth. Daphne and Aunt Phyllis, who was also from Jamaica, talked every day.

"Girl, me can't wait to tell you this. You will not believe it! No Sir! Must tell you!"

They had a very special relationship. Yet, my mother did not perceive Aunt Phyllis as Chinese, because culturally, they were just the same. The beautiful, tall, Chinese - Jamaican woman and the average height, Jamaican woman, were the same in my mother's heart.

She tried hard to connect me up with a Chinese man, but I would slip every time. You see, it is now twenty years after the first part of my book. I have never mentioned before how very smart I was and could act so dumb. It would make you shiver to know some of the things I could get out of by myself. I thank God for that part of my life. You see even though it was a beautiful day and hour when I landed from my mother's womb, I came out *fighting with a strong belief that God was with my every move.*

Well working helped me a lot and since my mother was a seamstress, it didn't take too long for me to get some clothes. She would even make over some of her dresses for me. So, I went to work, looking good then. I started night school at Tech High in Jamaica. It was fun. I also took Spanish lessons, typing. None of the two worked. I ended up being a good housekeeper. I still have no regrets.

***

Yes, I agree. My mother was a great housekeeper. She worked for the second generation of a wealthy family who treated her like a member of the family.

I remember meeting Dr. and Mrs. Brown, her new boss, when I was a little girl. Mrs. Brown was an artist, and she did volunteer work with the local museum. I recalled one of her projects: still life drawings of fruits and vegetables which she painted on the white cabinets of her kitchen like they were canvases. I thought that was remarkable. It took her more than a year to finish all those cupboard doors; but they were beautiful. She worked with oil paints; so sometimes, there was a whiff of that smell from her apron.

Once, while in her artist cottage, a short walk from the house, I watched as Mrs. Brown painted a nude. I was speechless, in awe of her work, as I stood in the doorway of the cottage, with my arm resting on the wooden door frame. I could smell oil from the paint, but it didn't bother me. A profusion of light saturated the room from the many windows. My eyes blinked involuntarily. The painting, a nude, in a reposing position, looked real, relaxed, content as she came to life on the canvas.

Mrs. Brown turned around. With a gentle smile she said, "Beverley, how long have you been standing there?"

I couldn't even answer, and momentarily forgot why my mother sent me to the cottage.

"Not long Mrs. Brown. My mother told me to remind you that Mrs. Nelson is coming for lunch today."

"Oh yes, that's right!"

The painting was beautiful. I did not want to leave the vision of the canvas, as Mrs. Brown returned to her work, taking her time with staunch attention to details. She added her sweet singing voice to the environment. Precious!

"Tell your mother, I'm coming. Thank you, Beverley."

Whenever I looked at Mrs. Brown, she always smiled with a thin, placid face. She rarely wore make-up and didn't wear fancy clothes. She made most of her dress clothes. She was casual and comfortable, sweet and endearing as the sound of her lovely voice penetrated the environment.

Dr. Brown was more mysterious to me. His face was kind with smooth skin, yet he had an air of gentle efficiency, never abrasive like someone I knew. He took charge and was nice to us. He was a doctor at the hospital. I remember one of my classmates being assigned to him, when she went in for an emergency. She didn't say much, other than she wasn't talking to him, so I have no idea of his personality at work. However, at home he actually listened to his children. They could tell him anything, unlike my father who thought whatever his children had to say was foolishness.

I loved visiting that white Colonial mansion, hidden neatly behind a grove of trees and foliage. The three-story mansion included a wine cellar and bomb shelter.

My mother took Norman and me down to see the bomb shelter one day. I was a little nervous, because of what the name denotes. But we followed my mother down wide cement stairs to the basement. There it was, next to a wine cellar - hobby room - where they made some of their own wines from grapes on their property, and fresh homemade strawberry ice-cream. Really delicious!

The room was amazing in a way, just to think you could be protected from bombs. Real live bombs that could destroy everything! It was like being in a tomb, because of all the concrete walls. There were air vents and tunnels to support your breathing, once the vast metal door was locked. I figured the doctor would be at the hospital, the older children in school, so only Mrs. Brown, my mother Daphne and the younger children would be there.

In the fifties, a regular monthly drill was the Civil Defense drill preparing us for the attacks from the Nazi's, the communists and whoever else was coming to get us here in America. It was on television and the radio. We heard the air-raid warning sound that seemingly went on forever and interrupted our favorite television shows.

I remember at school preparing for the bomb drills, where the entire class moved to the big hallways. This was a massive exercise. Initially we giggled, it seemed like fun and we didn't have to do school work. But then we realized this was serious: air raid drills at school where we dropped beneath our desks, and covered our heads with our arms, then moved to the halls. At school, war filmstrip footages were shown to us during social studies classes, where our teachers would try to explain what was going on. I guess our teachers did a good job, but all the filmstrips looked the same, you had to see the uniform to know who was coming after who.

As I knelt in the hallway in front of the lockers on my hands and knees, my head covered with my hands and arms for protection, I had a good feeling knowing that my mother was safe. She would be in the bomb shelter, with reinforced concrete, mortar and steel, at the mansion, with rations properly identified and supplies for the family of which she was part of. She would not get hurt and she had food and people who loved her, I thought as a smile ran through my mind. Yes, that made me feel good.

I also felt better with my childhood 'Bestest' friend, Betty, who was usually next to me; because Norman was a year older, so he was in a different class with his friends; and Orlando, five years older, was attending a different school. Periodically, I lifted my head during the drills and saw a sea of little bodies covered with coats on the floor, probably three rows deep, huddled against or near the lockers.

Betty and I walked to school every day and played at each other's houses. She was so much fun! We shared many joys, like dressing alike on Twin Days, buying sweaters alike at Christmas; and responsibilities at school over the years: classroom monitors, crossing guards for students for which we left class five minutes early – proudly wearing a white Patrol Belt and later earned metal badges as we advanced in status. In junior high, we hit the warning sounds – a small xylophone with a mallet, before ringing the bell between passing periods. This was another reason to leave class two minutes early. We were reliable and maintained excellent grades. We always made the honor roll. My life with Betty was filled with spontaneous laughter. We laughed at everything. Sometimes, we placed our hands on our stomachs, because we were laughing so hard.

During the drill, depending on the weather outside, we wore wool coats, hat and leggings, or cotton dresses, pants and sweaters. Oddly, no one had to go to the restroom.

Administrators and teachers were walking up and down the hallway checking on us and looking for spies, I supposed.

***

The mansion sat impressively on several acres of grassy flatland with a horseshoe shaped driveway leading to the massive front door. Four or five tall white columns lined the entry. The swimming pool was off the kitchen/garage and a natural lake was below the beveled glass windows of the dining room. The lake even though it was beautiful was a little eerie and dark. The water looked almost black. It was shaded by trees, tall trees bending over to embrace the water's surface. I remember Mrs. Brown telling me of an incident that happened there. She and my mother had to rescue one of the family dogs from the lake in the heart of winter; and Indianapolis had wicked, ugly winters. First, Mrs. Brown struggled with the animal in the frigid water. My mother seeing the pending catastrophe, came out and jumped in to help her. The two of them were finally able to hold on to the pet and drag him out. They had to take hot showers to restore their body temperatures, I suppose. Mrs. Brown even had to put the dog in the shower with her.

But the day, years later, when Mrs. Brown recalled the incident to me, she said, "Beverley, your mother was my best friend." I couldn't believe what she said.

"Yes, Beverley, it's true!" She repeated her statement.

Rightfully *Hers*

I never knew she felt that way about my mother. I knew of course that the children loved my mother, but I had no idea that Mrs. Brown did too.

A greenhouse, hot and humid, off the dining room, was where the owners planted interesting plant cuttings from all over the world. A large handsome library with leather/gold embossed books and big comfy upholstered chairs was just off the grand entry hall. At the end of the hall, just past the tall antique grandfather clock, were white double staircases with mahogany banisters leading to a walkway to the second floor. The mansion had a majestic living room with vintage oriental carpets and a grand piano. The sunroom next door with a ping pong stand and a pool table was my two older brothers' favorite room. Sometimes, Eddie and I played pool too. This was a little difficult for Eddie because he was a little boy. Sometimes, Orlando lifted him, a little awkward, but they managed to play the game.

This was the third job I could remember my mother having. The first one at the hospital cafeteria, my mother quit a couple of years later when they would not grant her leave to pick up her sick child at school. I believe that child was me. My mother said that she would never ask for leave again.

Her second job was part-time which she got through her church friend, Cletus. Cletus had an inverted triangular body shape, in other words she was large on top and, thin on the bottom. Her skin was fair like my mother's and she wore her hair in short curls they called a poodle haircut. She was smart though, definitely part of the new generation and knew a lot about many things, so she was a big help to my mother who had a lot to learn about life in America.

Cletus was a cook, more like a head chef. I could tell from the fancy dishes she prepared for the Big Brown family (that's what we called the doctor's parents) and dinner parties. Often, she needed additional help at the Big Brown's home, so she asked my mother to come and serve as a hostess. On other occasions, my mother was asked to prepare Jamaican meals for the guests. She prepared Jamaican fried chicken with fresh garlic, olive oil, onions and tomatoes, sometimes with curry, served with garden fresh sliced tomatoes, rice and black-eyed peas.

This second job had a lasting impression on me. One that is permanently cast in my memory. My father took Norman and me to this spectacular, custom built, log cabin home (never saw anything like this) to pick up my mother after church. She helped with clean-up after a large party on Saturday night, maybe once a month. Norman and I sat on a park bench next to this quiet, sleepy lake the family called Shangri-la. The lake was breath-takingly beautiful. I could see diamonds on the surface of the water, as I blinked my eyes, and tried to shade them from the sun. Between the lake and the magnificent log cabin home, we waited for our mother still dressed in our Sunday clothes. Sometimes, I would doze off, Norman too. One day our mother walked over to us and she said that she had a special treat for us, and it wasn't food.

Well, what could that be? Norman and I looked at each other, then eyed our mother. She did not keep us in suspense long. Our mother said it was an anti-gravity house, built on the property by the grandparents for the amusement of their grandchildren. Now this sounded interesting! I had never heard of such a house, but Orlando had been there with my mother, when he went to help on the farm land.

The little house was really hard to get into, because the forces of nature took over and prevented you from entering. We had to use all of our strength to propel our bodies towards the house; and once you got in, a force would thrust you into a padded wall. I had to again use all my energy to pull myself off the wall. Everything in the house was against the pull of gravity. There was water in there that went uphill instead of down. Wooden balls that rolled upwards instead of downwards. Unbelievable! This anti-gravity room was a pretty remarkable place. When I left the room, I was pretty exhausted, but absolutely elated!

Norman and I looked at each other, both laughing. "That is remarkable!" said Norman.

"Unbelievable," I said as we exchanged giant smiles, while trying to catch our breath.

Our mother continued as she approached, "Well, what did you think?" Her eyes were shiny in anticipation of our answers.

"That was really cool," said Norman.

I repeated, "Unbelievable," then added, "Fantastic!" as I stared at that little house that gave us so much pleasure.

***

I also joined the Kingston Parish Church in the heart of the city. It was a beautiful church and the Father there that I became acquainted with was Father Bateman. He was older, and Father Davis, was much younger and a very fine minister. Well I took part in Sunday School and the young people's choir. I really enjoyed both. Then I was asked to help with the Sunday School. I was also studying for Confirmation. I guess you would call that a kind of baptism. That is where I met my husband of 42 years. He said the thing he admired most was the way I answered questions that were asked of us in classes and I never missed a class.

The church has always played a great part in my life. Oh, how I am thankful to God for that. You see on Sundays, I was so good, I went there three times each Sunday and loved it. After Sunday School, which started at 3 p.m., we moved chairs to the back of the church, and we would all sit *around and talk. Many times, Father Davis would join us.*

At our home, after dinner, my mother would ask me to play her favorite hymns from church. She loved those hymns, "What a Friend We Have in Jesus," "Just as I Am," and "In the Garden," were a few of her favorites. Sometimes, she tried to play them herself, but she wasn't very good at it. So, I would walk over to the piano and play them for her. My father paid for music lessons for all his kids. We went weekly to the Jordan Conservatory of Music, but frankly, we did not take practicing seriously. My father's plan was that we would play piano in his church when we were older, and none of us wanted to do that. The hymns were easy for me. It was the more difficult classical music that I had trouble with.

I think one Sunday evening, Norman (my husband) rode up behind me and said, 'Good Evening.' We started a conversation. He asked if I was going back to night service. I said, 'Yes.' He said, 'Would it be okay if I picked you up?' Well, I said yes without even asking my mother. After we walked to my gate, he rode off. I really thought that he was a nice young man, the reason is: It's no different today, than in those days, not too many young men were getting on bicycles and riding to church two or three times each Sunday.

I remember my aunt's stepmother telling me to try always to get a husband who goes to church. That stayed with me through the years.

***

My mother's voice was soft like that of a schoolgirl talking about her boyfriend or one who was excited about the prospects of a new relationship, but didn't want to jinx it.

***

"We were seeing each other regularly. He would even come to my work place. I introduced him to everyone. By this time at work, I got close to my boss, Mrs. Howell. She was a fine woman and would tell me right from wrong. I could ask any questions and she would try to answer them. My backbone was Father Davis. I could tell him all my troubles and when he got through lecturing me, everything was fine.

Norman's friendship and mine blossomed just beautifully; but for some reason or other, my mother had to move as she was always doing, because she didn't want to pay the rent. There were little things here and there that Norman *didn't like about my mother, especially mother's cursing. She was a real town bully and she could draw a crowd anywhere.*

She used to cook and would offer Norman dinner, but after a while I think she just wanted more. She thought that he should be giving me some money. As usual, that was always the starting point. So, things were not working out well.

After that, we would meet at church and plan to go to the park, take a walk or see a movie; but he never left me alone. He was always there no matter what, until one night when my mother decided that she had had enough of him, she let him have 'her tongue.' I was never so embarrassed in my life. He left.

I remember bits and pieces of that conversation with my grandmother's voice ringing loudly in Daphne's ear as Phyllis shouted at the top of her lungs to my father.

"You thinks you smart man? Smarter than me, her mother, ya hear? Listen me! Me no have to have no stinking man in this house. No – mother-fucking - stinking - man!..."

I realize how devastating those words were on the heart of a young lady who had acquired clothes, which her mother made, so that she could go to church, presentable, and church was where she met my father. Those words stripped every piece of clothing she acquired, as well as the confidence gained from being with people who supported her. Again, she stood figuratively naked in the midst of this verbal degradation as she had done a lifetime before, with her mean aunt.

***

I watched my mother pull a tissue from her pocket. The ritual begins again. The memory of that day flashed like an Indian summer over her heated brow. Phyllis' cold and callous words burned deep into her heart, just as if she been branded with a piping hot wrought iron. She wiped the moisture from her forehead, while the heat boiling below the surface of her skin rose to blistering levels. She looked casually into the distance. My eyes followed her for a moment, then looked around. It was as if I wasn't in the room.

Her eyes dry now, she continued.

"I thought that I would never see him again. I cried all night."

She paused, took a deep breath and tears again neared the narrow perimeter of her eyes. She returned to the script that was sealed in the temple of her mind, like hieroglyphics on a cave wall. Her voice assumed a confidence previously lacking.

"The next morning when I heard his bicycle bell, I couldn't believe it. Even the other tenants were

surprised. He never came inside again, however. He would always wait for me outside. One day on the way to work he said to me, 'You are a lily in a stagnant pool and I'm going to take you right out of it....' I don't think I'll ever forget that either."

My mother often repeated that metaphor especially when it was important for her to remember the gentle man who captured her heart and plucked her from a stifling life; for that she would be forever grateful to my father. He was so different now, she said; but I remember that he often spoke poetically, using references from the Bible to support his position, as Assistant Pastor in our church. The black churches in America are places where black men could express themselves and openly share their knowledge.

These words taken from First Corinthians always held a special meaning for me when you talk about love, and my father used these verses frequently in his church sermons.

1   Though I speak with the tongues of men and of angels, and have not love, I am only a resounding brass or tinkling cymbal.

2   And though I have the gift of prophecy, and understand all mysteries, and all knowledge; and though I have all faith, so that I could remove mountains, and have not love, I am nothing.

3   Though I bestow all my goods to feed the poor, and though I give my body to be burned, and have not love, it profiteth me nothing.

4   Love suffereth long, and is kind, love envieth not, love vaunteth not itself, is not puffed up.

5   Doth not behave itself unseemly, seeketh not her own, is not easily provoked, thinketh no evil...."

These words my father quoted from the Bible, were so powerful, so beautiful, yet so compelling, could bring me to tears. He spoke these words. They spilled out from his mouth, freely, with such meaning and passion! I wanted to believe that he understood what these words meant, but I was never sure. Actions speak louder than words.

Yes, this was my father - the man who quoted poetry from Shakespeare at his blue collar work place talent shows, and you know how well that went over; who more often than not ended his church sermons in "Silver and gold have I none, but such that I have, give I thee, in the name of Jesus Christ arise and walk." This was one of his favorite biblical references, which he quoted whether it fit his text or not.

'You are a lily in a stagnant pool,' my mother uttered softly, reflectively, almost like a prayer. My mother never wore liquid foundation, just a little lipstick and powder. Yet during those times, when she repeated his words, her face glowed like that radiant bell-shaped flower floating reverently on still waters. That was the man my mother saw in my father. I wanted to meet that person. Really get to know him, the gentle man, sensitive, caring man. Where was he?

Conversely, I thought my mother, the beautiful Lily, was riding the rapids with safe return not a guarantee as our family life grew more complex. Help from my father would come, if and only if, it benefited him to do so. Had he plucked a lily from a stagnant pool and grown tired of its beauty or like a child, was no longer interested? Saving the lily no longer suited his purpose. This really puzzled me and the reminders of the lily in the stagnant waters were forever present each time I sat quietly around the fishpond in our backyard. I would look at the majestic pink and white flowered heads above leathery green shiny pads, and watched tiny green frogs jumping from pad to pad, wondering about my parents, our lives in general, while taking in the beauty around me. This area my father made us weed and clean weekly through his child-labor practices. "It's a Dandy," he would say. Yes, reminders were always present.

There were many times that I selected to sit next to the lily pond, and certainly other times, I was directed to sit by the pond by my father.

"You kids need some fresh air. Take a book and go outside…. I don't want to hear anything more!"

It was peaceful, quiet, and engaging in a subtle way. I watched life take place in and around the pond. In the springtime, I saw jellied bubbles, eggs really, attached to the side of the pond or a pad of the water lily. I later watched as tadpoles developed and swam around. Then the actual frogs, tiny ones, but full grown, appeared on the lily pads, hopping from pad to pad. Seemingly, enjoying their afternoon, as I enjoyed watching them; until of course, I heard the loud buzzing of a yellow jacket. Then, it would appear, from nowhere, and spoil everything. I took off running. I wasn't going to let the big bug bite me. I guess in a way, my mother wasn't going to take the bite from my father either.

Ironically, it was my father who restored hope in my mother, not my grandmother. I liked this part of her story, so I was a little anxious as to how she would proceed.

"Well in the next few days, my mother didn't have much to say. It wouldn't have done any good anyway, because she knew by then I was hardheaded, and I didn't mind dying as long as he cared that much to come back. I intended to keep on going out with him. Also, there were a few folks around who told her they thought the best thing to do was to leave us alone. She was really bitter though. Anyway, the following Sunday he came to pick me up for Sunday school. When I got outside, he said, 'I have something for you,' and handed me a small box. I could hardly *open it. I was shaking. It was a beautiful engagement ring."*

I looked at the wedding ring my mother wore, a gold band. I helped to remove it a number of times when her fingers were swollen during pregnancies. The engagement ring was not there, but I saw that ring with the two diamond chips to the side of the center diamond in my mind. It was dull in comparison, but nothing a little jewelry cleaner could not correct. I imagine what it looked like when my mother opened the velvet box. It must have transformed into the property of the Queen of England, a ring from the Crown Jewels. Yes, I am sure of that.

"He just took it from me and slipped it on my left finger and I flew back into the house like a crazy fool just screaming. Everyone came out running and I was saying,....' look at my engagement ring from Norman. Isn't it beautiful!' The tears are running down my face, but it seems everyone else was crying too. While we ooo-ed and ah-ed, he was still standing there waiting for me. I had my face fixed up and went back out. We headed for church to find Father Davis to tell him the news first, then the rest of our friends and the Sunday school class.

Chapter 6

I think it was the first part of the year and we decided to plan a June wedding. By this time mother had written to my father about this bad guy she couldn't get me away from and he wrote back to say he would help her. He didn't scare me any. I was tough, so I sent to tell him about my engagement. I don't know how he and mother made out. It really didn't matter. We made up our minds. It was OK with me if they wanted to go along, fine. If they didn't, still finer. We were going to get married and it seems as if the whole town was behind us. Things settled down quite a bit, but I don't think until this day, Norman trusted my mother anymore.

We had a beautiful wedding. It was about 1 ½ hours late, because I waited for Father Davis. He had been transferred far away, but he came back *to marry us. Everything was lovely and Dad was real proud of me."*

I thought about the wedding from stories my mother, grandmother and aunt collaborated. My grandmother and my aunt, Lolita, my father's sister, made her wedding dress. They were professional seamstresses. The dress had a long flowing majestic train and was hand beaded. My grandfather used his connections at work to provide safety and a regal atmosphere at the wedding. Constables in Dress-whites on horses and in cars lined the street and entrance to the magnificent doors of the Episcopalian church. One would have thought that the wedding was for the daughter of a dignitary. If my grandparents had never done anything for their daughter, Daphne, in her life, they made sure this day was one she would never forget.

***

This was the first time in my mother's story that my grandfather became a real person. My mother's chosen words were, 'Dad was real proud of me.' I know she should have said "'really' proud of me." But this is my mother's story. Nevertheless, their relationship sounded personal with warmth as if she really knew him, not just a name on a letter she saw bundled among her aunt's papers in her bedroom, or money in white envelopes mailed to her monthly; or better yet - the memory of that precious dress her father sent, which was too small. She loved the dress anyway, because it was hers.

Her little four-year old cousin, confused by the gift, said to her, "Why him buy you a little one?"

But she held on to that dress her father sent. Held it close to her heart, soft like a baby's breath, not the harsh jute sack she was wearing. That was until her aunt took it from her and probably sold it to a neighbor.

I don't remember meeting my maternal grandfather, but it seems as if my mother knew him. Without even a photograph of him, I sense the sound of his voice and pictured him over and over in my mind from my mother's account of him. He was a policeman, a constable. His most prominent features were like those of my mother - yellow colored skin, freckles and red hair. My most dramatic recollection of my grandfather was when I joined my mother at our dining room table. I was twelve years old at the time.

"What's wrong mother? Why are you crying?" My mother sat quietly at the end of the mahogany table, not an expensive one, but large enough to accommodate her children. She didn't answer, but tears made their way gently down a tired, placid face. She just returned from work, picking up mail. She held a letter in her hand. I knew it was from Jamaica, because I could see the veined thin bluest-cast paper with red, white and blue airmail wings between her fingers. She barely looked up, then handed me the thin envelope that opened into a letter serving a dual function. I looked at the envelope, opened the flap, and read the contents. Sitting in the chair next to her, I immediately got up and moved to put my arms around my mother's firm upper shoulders. She remained seated.

"He's dead," my mother said in an exhausted whisper. She inhaled, then exhaled. "I had so much to tell him, and he's dead." She gazed into the ceiling, "God, why didn't I get a chance to tell him." She seemed so fragile initially, then I sensed anger as she repeated herself.

"What did you want to tell him?" I asked quietly. What could it be? Now tears trickled down my own face for the grandfather I didn't even remember meeting, yet honestly felt like I had, probably as an infant and toddler. Never saw a picture of him! But mostly, the tears were for my mother. She sat, quietly heaving in pain, for what seemed like an eternity, unable to speak.

My mother broke the deafening silence when she uttered softly between weighed sobs, "I wanted to tell him that he was my father after all. I wanted to hear from him...." Tears poured profusely down my mother's face. I, in quiet support, just waited.

"Damn it to hell," my mother shouted. "He was my father!"

Her voice, rising now, as the inferno fueled the hurt from years past. I placed my hand on her hand, feeling the warmth beneath my skinny fingers. Waited! Then she slipped her hand away, and said stiffly, "It was not my duty to write....He was my father for God's sake!...for God's sake!"

Her voice drifted off as she repeated over and over, like the rhythm of a rosary.

"He was my father, after-all. He was my father, after-all...."

The last letter my mother received from her father said in his best Jamaican/ British tradition, 'It is your duty to write your father, whether I answer or not.' That letter was two years before. My mother did not share that content with me. She just went about her life, taking care of her family.

After the death of her father, my mother never mentioned my grandfather again to me. I never asked questions about him, because I did not want to make her sad. It was clear to me, from seeing my mother's raw physical and emotional response that day, that my mother really loved her father. She was desperate for him to be in her life and was totally devastated by his death. With him, she had a real chance for fraternal love. I don't think he was spoiled as Phyllis was by the gifts, expectations and demands of a well-to-do family. In fact, my grandmother Phyllis told me that he came to the house to ask her father for her hand in marriage.

My grandmother words: "Me was frightened, you know Mistress Bev. Me hear the commotion between me father and Mr. Steven. But him said, he wanted to marry me. Me hear that good! Cook, (head housekeeper and cook) blocked me path. Me about six/seven months pregnant at the time. Not quick on me feet! She would not let me go to him. Me hear my father yell, 'Ya ever come back here, Me KILL ya! Ya hear what me say. Me KILL you! Me promise you that.'"

"Cook believed what him say, as she whispered, her breath hot in me face, 'Him kill him.' Me looked out the window and watched as Mr. Steven take off, dust clouds covering his figure.... Cook repeated, 'Him kill him. It a matta of honor, ya understand? Ya honor!'"

"So many things happening Mistress Bev, ya see," my grandmother said as she moved her head back and forth in denial. "But next thing me know, me caunt have anything to do with the child, ya mother; and me shipped off to Cuba to live with relatives. They say me shamed the family."

This experience eventually led to Phyllis disowning her only child, angry by the major change in her young life and later blaming that child, my mother, for all her unhappiness. I knew that my mother would have to reconcile these issues on her own. If that were ever possible.

I would have liked to have known my grandfather, however. I have pictured him, yellow colored with freckles like my mother. My grandmother Phyllis said, "Him yellow, child. Ya' mother favors him." I visualized him in the dress whites of his constable uniform, providing helpful instructions with a smile or directives, when necessary, with a stern, yet determined demeanor. How he died was also of interest to me. Was it a work-related injury? I never pursued a Hall of Records inquiry or Ancestry.com. Maybe someday!

***

This duty obligation, "It is your duty to write to your father, whether I answer or not," was also used by my own father. 'It is your duty to be a good student. It is your duty to be a good daughter. It is your duty...." Well, what was his duty? I knew of course – he provided, kept a roof over our heads, but he had no duty to be kind.

***

I was in my forties, visiting Indiana. It was a lovely Sunday afternoon dinner which the family used to catch up on our lives, when I asked my father, "Why were you so mean to us as children? My father looked up from his dinner plate, so did my brothers and sisters. Norman's look said, "Why Bev?" Even my husband Clarence eyed me. My question immediately changed the mood at the table. My father slowly put his knife and fork down, braced his large shoulder against the host chair, then took a breath, speaking with confidence.

"I was mean to you kids to make you good. See how good you all turned out," he gestured with his hands outstretched as he looked around the table. I sat there, immobile. I couldn't believe what he just said. 'No apology. No, I'm sorry!'

Orlando burst out laughing, Norman followed with a nervous mirth, then my younger siblings. Our father then laughed hardily too. Proud of himself! My mother looked at me, not wanting me to spoil this rare family time together. So, I didn't say anything else. I was frozen in the time I spent with my father, perplexed beyond belief, knowing my father in his mind had validated his behavior towards his children in this mindless way, and felt justified in doing so. After all, look at the great results he got: six successful children.

***

Tears shielded my mother the day she received the news of her father's death, the day of reckoning. The child within her shouted emphatically and boastfully, "Damn it! It is not my duty! Do you hear me? It is not my duty. Damn it to hell!"

The sound was clearly expelled from my mother's lips and the words were unquestionably intended for my grandfather, Steven Edward, but he was not there, only me.

After that letter from two years before, my mother never wrote to her father again believing in a childlike way she didn't need him. He was not there to support her as a child. Possibly, she negated his money sent monthly. Afterall, what child would choose money over a loving relationship with her father? She made it this far without him - all the way to America. Yet, the cold hard consequence Daphne had to accept, however, was that she never heard from him again, nor he from her. The two were probably more alike than different. Two years of pain magnified rage in monumental proportions within the heart of this gentle woman. The child within her, without a doubt, suffered again, irrefutable damage.

***

The sound of the front door closing caught my attention. Looking up, I saw my older brothers, and I was really glad to see them. Orlando said, "What's wrong," as he and Norman joined me in consoling my mother. I handed Orlando the letter. Now our mother was braced against three of her children for support, the three who traveled with her to America.

I intended to ask Orlando if he remembered our grandfather, because this man on the peripheral of my life, my mother's father, was merely a picture in my mind. But as life went on, I never did. Orlando, five years older than me, would remember our grandfather best. He actually knew him.

***

"I mean I had everything! I wish I had a picture to show. It was a large wedding and afterwards we danced till dawn. Only one thing staying still vivid in my mind, I was so tired. I didn't take off my gown at all. It was pinned up on hooks that held the train and I really danced. We didn't go on a honeymoon. The next day we really enjoy just opening our gifts, which were plenty.

My mother told me that no one remembered to bring a camera to the wedding. So, she described for me the best she could that special day in her life. My thoughts vividly blew up as my mind filtered her information through my senses. It sounded so beautiful!

Ironically, Daphne said she remembered being overwhelmingly tired the day of her wedding. This child was up before the chickens crowed, and the rising sun, and walked five miles with no shoes to her aunt's husband's store to take him his lunch. Yet, on her wedding day, she was tired. The same feeling from her horrible childhood. Yes, she was tired, emotionally tired, from others doing for her instead: Her mother, and future sister-in-law, spent months on her hand-beaded wedding dress; her father got his fellow comrades from the police force to add a special flare and safety, as well as walked her down the aisle in his Dressed White uniform; Father Davis, rode for miles in a horseback carriage to get to her wedding where he would officiate; neighbors, friends, her father's money and the church provided all the food and beverages, and friends from her Sunday school provided the music that they dance to.

She also waited for her 'showers of blessings.' This is a symbolic belief that God sends a gift of rain bestowing his wishes for a successful marriage. The showers came that day, just a light one, but assuring my mother that her marriage was sanctioned by God.

***

Our marriage was a good one. I got pregnant and it was another turn in my life, yes children. Our first baby, however, was stillborn. After two days of labor, I went to a private nursing home. I don't really know what happened. She was a large baby, and all I know is that the nurse did not call the doctor. They claimed that I had labored too long. Oh, my beautiful baby never lived. There was a little part of me that went with her."

My mother sighed. A shadow encompassed the soft mounds of her cheekbones as they lost color, like the moon passing in front of the sun. She blinked slowly and inhaled deeply as if it were her last breath or more importantly, the fresh sweet breath of her baby.

"I can tell you, it's no fun carrying a baby for nine months and going home empty handed. They did not let me see her after she was dressed. They just took her away and buried her. Oh, that was a little cruel."

A lone tear mounted the lower lid of my mother's right eye and tumbled like a cotton ball over the familiar path of her face, landing gracefully on her left hand. The gold wedding band caught my eye as the tear neared its circumference. It symbolized the union of my parents. Ironically, my father never once mentioned the daughter he lost, and my mother never forgot her. She would be my big sister. I would have loved that.

Chapter 7

"Well things went along fine, but my one ambition was wanting another baby. There were times when I wondered a lot. Suppose I didn't get pregnant again? It happened so many times to other women. One thing for sure, I just had to have children. I just couldn't see a home without children. So, with the help of God, yes very soon after, I was expecting again. Oh, I was going to take good care of myself. I still wanted to go back to the nursing home again. I didn't want to go to the hospital.

In the meantime, war broke out in America and they were taking men from everywhere and Norman left to work in Panama for the war effort. Norman was a tailor and worked for a store on Harbor Street in Jamaica. The store was named Vanity Fair. He made good money in those days, but then the traveling fever came and suddenly he decided to go to Panama to work for the United

States of America. Well, there was nothing I could do about the situation. He was leaving and I was very sad, but my one comfort was that I was expecting. The pregnancy would keep me busy and I look forward to his letters. They would give me a lot of hope.

My father was without question an outstanding tailor. Girls were assigned Home Economics in school in the fifties and sixties, where sewing was required. I didn't know that boys could sew. They directed American boys into shop classes, not sewing or even foods. I did not hear of Vanity Fair until I was a teenager. Not sure if it was the same company. But the work my father did was remarkable!

Clients came to our home for fittings, the women were a little plump – pear/round shaped, the men on the taller side with medium frames. Sometimes, the ladies were standing in the dining room in full length nylon slips, and stockings of course. Showing beneath the slips were the stays of their long line brassieres (Stays are plastic tubing material stitched into the bra covering to keep the fabric in place). Thick shoulder straps dangled down heavy arms and high waisted girdles with long spandex legs supported their short stocky ones.

My father stood next to them making assessments with his yellow measuring tape hanging from his thick neck. He then leaned over to write the numbers on a pad on the table. He was very professional. The ladies were like mannequins to him.

He could make anything; but oddly, he never invited me in to watch or to help. I just peeped from the kitchen door, as he worked.

Once I saw him make a man's suit completely by hand, even making his own tissue pattern, with tailor tacks, stitches, wax and chalk markings everywhere. The fabrics, linings and tracing papers were spread out on the large dining table, which looked like an algebraic problem with geometry on chalk boards in classrooms. I watched him bring this fabric to life.

***

Things changed a little and mother and I became friends again she was also good help to me. I decided to move into a larger apartment with my mother. Norman didn't like that at all, but I said to him, 'She's my mother. I think we'll make it this time.' Well things didn't work out too well. I think my mother was jealous. Whenever I get my money which was from Norman, mother was always mad. I guess she just did not like to see me handling the money. There was a blowout between us, and I decided to move back to his family, which I hated, but I wasn't going to let anyone run my life anymore. Mother and I never spoke again, *until after three years or more. I saw her a few times and just kept on walking."*

When my mother actually told me about the number of times, she saw her mother and said nothing, she was sad. I could tell right away. Pretending that she did not know this woman, my grandmother, was initially hard for her. But each time, she remembered the pain her mother brought into her life.

My mother's emotions seemingly unwound like a spool of iridescent gold thread running the length of a long, worn carpet. The color at the center of her face while immensely intense initially, diluted over the soft bones of her flushed cheeks. The China doll in the shadowbox of the entry hall came at once to my mind. There was an unusual connection between that small porcelain doll figurine and my mother, whom I adored.

My fascination with that China doll captured me in a quietly passionate way. The doll had a smudge of crimson across her cheeks, glazed brown eyes, creamy beige skin tone and golden-brown ringlets hanging like pitted olives beneath her lacy bonnet. Her delicate smile and pointed chin, emitted a subtle air of confidence. She wore a party dress with layers of starch Chantilly lace gathered from the waist to the hem of the skirt. Her outfit mirrored a gathered lace pink Easter dress of mine that I loved to wear. My neighbor even asked me to wear that dress when I was a flower girl in her wedding. I was older, so I was more like a Junior Bride's maid.

I just loved to spin that figurine on its base, where her legs, ankles, and shoes narrowed into a thumb-size porcelain vertex.

I watched the images of the China doll transform as it swirled. One day I went through my usual preoccupation of twirling the doll, when the doll, absorbing the centrifugal force, toppled over, striking the blacktop of the credenza beneath it.

I made a frantic attempt to catch her, but useless, as the porcelain doll exploded into pieces before my eyes. The pounding in my chest slammed the edifice of my mind, charging me with the destruction of an innocent soul.

The barrister of my thoughts challenged me, 'Did you destroy the doll you claim to love?' Thinking first, before I answered, I knew I had to save that doll.

"Mother is going to get you," the barrister of my thoughts said. 'No,' I wanted to say.

I turned and looked into Norman's face. It was Norman talking.

"You're always messing with that doll. Now look what you've done. I'm gonna' tell mother."

Norman's words bounced off the white walls, like the doll vaulting off the black credenza, reverberated in my ears and returned to the insidious opening in the pit of my stomach. I knew that Norman would not tell. If our mother was told, I would do it. We did not tell on each other, a matter of unwritten agreement between siblings. Besides, our mother had more serious concerns, so we didn't bother her with small matters.

Nervously, I picked up each piece, handling the particles delicately like precious stone. I was determined to reconstruct the doll's beauty. The tedious process began. Norman helped me. We found all the glue around the house, Elmer's glue, and Orlando's two-inch tubes of airplane glue that he used for his model planes. If I succeeded, I silently vowed from that day forward, my fascination with that China doll would be solely from a distance.

When I finished, I examined my work with Norman's help. I slowly turned the doll ever so carefully in the carousel, created in the palm of my hand. All the breaks were patched, barely noticeable. We used clear nail polish to smooth out the rough surfaces, and to give it a shiny surface. I was again satisfied with the rhapsody of the doll's charm. It could still hold a special place in my heart.

Somehow, I thought my mother was a delicate reflection of that porcelain doll, beautiful on the outside, but broken on the inside. I ponder from time to time, 'Did my grandmother damage the life of her only child, destroying within her any chance for sustained happiness?'

***

One day I received a letter from her asking, if she could come and see the children. I didn't want to even answer the letter. Norman's mother talked to me, and after a good cry, I took Mammy's word and wrote back, and invited her to come and see us.

We waited for our mother to join us again. A pensive mood captured the life of the room and drained us of energy. The bedroom was hot and sticky now, almost stifling even though it was cool outside as a feathery breeze blew through the branches of the maple tree. My girlfriends and I agreed that the tree looked like an upside-down lady. I heard the melodic wind-song of a tingling Chinese glass wind chime playing the evening's overture. My father bought the wind chime the year before. I remember receiving the box when it came to our home. There was a picture of rectangular glass pieces with red Chinese painted letters. When my father removed it from the box, the wind chime looked exactly like the picture. In the wind, when the pieces gently touched, it created a harmonic resonance that flooded the backyard, making it enchanting.

"Now, my mother was so surprised because there were three children: Orlando the eldest, Norman and Beverley, the youngest. It worked out nicely, because she went home and on her next visit, she brought some pretty dresses for Bev that she had made herself.

Well, life went on. Norman was now in America. Things are going fine, only that we were drifting apart, and he was talking more and more about making America his home. Many men were still leaving, and many were sending back for their families. So now this was really something to look forward to. But there was always a doubt whether

115

the rest of the family would make it. Many families didn't. He did come home and made all the plans. I couldn't wait for the day to come when I would set foot on American soil."

I saw a tender gleam of remembrance in my mother's eyes and felt its gripping hold on her voice. She was mesmerized by the excitement of a new experience, a new exploration, hope reborn. The anticipation was good for the soul like a child waiting for a birthday party with all the preparations stimulating the senses as the celebration slowly squeezes another year, which the child willingly exchanges just to blow out those candles on the cake.

Daphne's children were the delay in her joining her husband in America. Determined not to have her own neglected childhood reflected in the confused eyes of her children, she would not leave Jamaica without them. No degree of coaxing and promises from her husband or in-laws could persuade her to leave without them. If and when she arrived in America, her three children would be with her.

"Oh boy, I did. It was wonderful when we all stepped off that plane. You see, the day I left Saint Thomas all by myself, I said there had to be a better life somewhere. Later, even though I was married with three children, Daphne was still searching for the better life somewhere."

116

Rightfully *Hers*

Each time my mother tasted the bitter - sweet of independence meshed with optimism, she used her name. "Daphne was still searching," she said - through the borrowed hopes of that wounded child - for a better life. My mother said, "…we all…." I knew that included my two brothers and me, because we were with her when she came to America.

***

I recalled the better life was hard coming, and we would remember for a lifetime the harsh winter of welcome when we arrived in the blurred mist of our mother's hope. That winter, cold penetrated not only our bodies, but also, our hearts.

***

"Mother, there goes Eddie again." The words came from Norman, but I instinctively jumped up as my mother closed the chapter on her life story. I knew that we would have to pick up where we left off with the reading the next day.

Eddie was sleepwalking again. A phenomenon that I thought was really strange, yet mysteriously interesting. My younger brother never remembered any of the incidents while sleepwalking. "That boy is crazy," Norman said, as our mother motioned for him to be quiet saying "Shhhhh," with a finger in front of her lips.

Our mother never woke Eddie on his sleep excursions. She told my brothers and me to just follow him around to make sure that he didn't get hurt. Sometimes his trips were very short. He just stood in our hallway like a statue or leaned against the painted plaster surfaces as if he was an extension of the wall. I watched him very carefully, taking my responsibility very seriously. Norman, on the other hand, would stifle his laughs or giggles under his breath, but this night would be a long outing.

Our little brother, Eddie, moved slowly down the hall, away from his shared bedroom. His balance was usually good, and he had a sense of direction, selectively choosing his way. He stopped briefly at the top of the stairs. We knew instinctively, he was going down. Norman ran in front of him as Eddie made his dissent. Norman had a mischievous laughter in his eyes. I, on the other hand, was dull for lack of a better word, never as animated as my older brother by one year. Mother-like was my behavior, as was taught and expected. I followed behind Eddie as our mother looked on.

Eddie was otherwise a neat little person, I believed. He was thoughtful and courteous and really very bright, making excellent grades in school. Ironically, he had an old soul. He understood life well for such a little rascal. He knew that he had an intricate part in our lives.

He looked so cute in his little shorts and khaki pants with large safari pockets and knee-length socks, and for a little guy he never really got very dirty. But here we were following Eddie on another one of his excursions down the steps. He went slowly, but not trance-like. Norman was going down the stairs backwards, watching Eddie but really enjoying not knowing what would happen next. Our foursome was focused on the dissent, when the front door opened. I saw my older brother Orlando. He whispered, "Not again!" We all nodded. Orlando waited until Eddie passed by. There was no recognition on Eddie's part that any of us were present. His eyes were always closed, but his destinations were somehow predetermined, not consciously of course, but he definitely knew where he was going.

I smiled to myself thinking, 'Wouldn't it be something if we were all asleep and Eddie was the only one awake? No, no way,' I thought.

Orlando went to the living room and turned on the television, as Eddie's tour group continued. The little rascal walked through the main entry hall, which I thought was wasted space in our home construction, directly into the dining room. He stood at the dining table, but didn't sit down. He just stood there. Then he swayed suddenly to the right. Norman, being closer, tried to catch him while spontaneously saying, "Whoa!"

I was tickled by Norman's quick action, but played it off well. Eddie wasn't awakened by his own sudden movements nor Norman's outburst with stifled laughter. Eddie slowly turned around retracing his steps. He waited at the bottom of the stairs for a little bit. He, then, started his assent.

Going up the steps, he was not as steady. Norman and I were balancing Eddie between us, as our mother followed behind. Norman was trying really hard not to laugh, his right eyebrow arched high on his forehead. I could see that tears were collecting in my brother's eyes from suppressed laughter; and

I could feel my own stomach muscles tighten as I suppressed my own.

When Eddie finally made it back to his bedroom, the bedroom he shared with his brothers, our mother stayed with him until she was reasonably certain he would not stir again. Norman and I ran down the steps swiftly, skipping steps in the quiet manner our father expected, but with laughter bellowing out where it belonged.

Chapter 8

Probably about five years old while sitting on a parson bench, badly in need of refinishing, I looked out the window of our house at a gray consuming sky. Wrapped in an oxblood wool coat, with a brown fur collar, and matching leggings my father bought me when I first arrived in Indiana in 1950, I sat quietly watching my breath crystallize on the window before my face, captivating really. He also selected a snuggly warm white muff ensemble for me with a soft fabric lining that covered my ears and hands. I loved the furry coordinated snowy white muff, with the face of a white rosy cheeked doll nestled comfortably in the center which kept my hands nice and cozy. The best gift was, I carried my doll with me everywhere I went, which always made me very happy.

But that day in November of 1951, I wasn't happy. I touched the smooth face of the doll as I listened nervously to the sound of my mother crying softly in the background. I was disheartened, because my mother was sad.

A small dining room entombed us with four slightly beat-up mint green plastic chairs and an old Formica table trimmed in chrome with chrome legs, which had lost their luster. My two older brothers were quiet as well. The gloom on their faces paralleled the muted shades of gray so common to

Indiana winters and was indicative of this day that left its debilitating presence as seemingly an omen to our life in America.

An emotional unbearable frost, left on the heels of my father's scheme that backfired, permeated the core of the duplex. My father thought he was clever. His approach to common renting practices in Indiana did much to further erode our mother's fragile persona. Our father rented a dark and narrow duplex, partially furnished. Like a rabbit trying to outsmart a fox, he slyly told the landlord that the unit would have two occupants, himself and his wife. When the landlord learned of his three children, the utilities were turned off, except for water.

It was Christmas time and the turkey donated by the church had to be prepared elsewhere. Our mother wept. She cried not so much because we were cold, she couldn't cook and we had to find another place to live; but more importantly those tears were for her husband's denial of the heart and sweet breath of their children, ...her lifeline.

Our father seemed sad as well. He could barely look at us. He saw the disappointment in the eyes of his children. Our mother's eyes were down, and her tears were enough for him. He had to make other arrangements. He didn't even say 'good-bye' when he left the house. We watched him trying to leave in his car. The driveway was packed with snow and ice beneath. A neighbor came to help him get the car out of the icy driveway. The car rolled back and forth, as the engine revved, then idled off. I could hear the car motor and see the wheels spinning like blowing into a windmill toy, but with ice, dirt and snow spurring from its sides.

I was nervous watching this scenario, but this action would become a natural part of our winters, always stuck in snow and ice. Orlando and neighbors helped to get cars out.

***

"How could he?" My mother mumbled and repeated through sobs, over and over, like a flashing neon sign barely visible in a snowstorm, while tears of despair soaked the white monogrammed handkerchief belonging to my father.

"They're all I have." Her recapitulation stacked up like dominoes on the verge of a fall.

With the exception of our mother's lament, the house and it was just a house, was void of sound - as it was void of heat and love. This rejection by my father only exacerbated the winter of my parents' discontent into a lifelong struggle that neither survived emotionally.

My mother was beclouded by my father's conscious renunciation of his children, and she envisioned even greater perils reading through and beyond his initial motivation. The denial was yet another stinging slap in the face of that injured child, denied all her life.

His children, wrapped in the epidermis of winter, sat in hushed, chilly, silence. Our minds lost in a vast cathedral of stain glass emotions, not sure if we should have come to this new country where landlords didn't like children and our own father disowned us when it was convenient, or if we should have remained behind in the comfort of our grandparent's home on the small island of Jamaica. Ironically, my mother wondered the same when she left her mean aunt's home to live with her mother, Phyllis, whom she didn't know harbored such hatred for her as well.

It's taken me more than fifty years to try to understand housing discrimination in the 50's, particularly those against families. AND I STILL DON'T UNDERSTAND IT! The laws intended to hurt, and our family was among those who suffered. Needless to say, there were many.

I am not sure what else our father could have done. He was new here as well, and he never had a family with him. It was clear that he did not understand the laws either. But we were living in a 'Jim Crow' city. Who knows if the renting practices were the same for black families as they were for white families? My father certainly did not identify with black families in America. He was different.

I suppose the real reason is that I am still angry about Jim Crow laws. I didn't even know that life was different for people who looked like me in other cities and states. I was quite suspicious of the laws and practices. But more so, I was disappointed with myself, for not knowing. I thought everyone in America lived like this. What was it about me and people who looked like me that drove white people to treat us this way?

When we went shopping on Saturdays, my mother's favorite past time, I held my urine, because the 'Colored only' toilets were so filthy. No one cleaned them, even though you had to pay to use them. I stood outside the door entrance with the packages, as the stench permeated the small halls. I wasn't walking in there and messing up my shoes. No way! My mother maneuvered floors laden with water from stopped up toilets and wet tissues. She could manage these nasty facilities, because she could squat.

I heard her yell from the stall, "Are you okay Beverley?"

"Yes Mother," I hollered back.

Even the water fountains for people who looked like me, were not clean. My mother would buy a Pepsi or coca cola, rather than have us drink from those rusty, dirty, low pressured basins, where the water barely passed the lip of the opening.

As a child, I wondered who was Jim Crow, anyway? Someone who hated children, particularly colored children! I wondered why my family had such a hard time renting, when my father had the money to pay. Was he the wrong color? Or when they actually met him, they heard his accent, and they probably said to themselves, 'He's not one of them.'

"Where are you from," they asked politely, yet inquisitively.

My father, I am sure, presented a big smile and said proudly, "I am from Kingston, Jamaica, British West Indies." I saw him do this a number of times, because people were always curious about his accent.

He and my mother were acceptable, but they did not want any of their progeny.

I thought back to kindergarten, when we had "Little Black Sambo" puzzles. The pieces were heavy, made of wood, and painted in bright colors. I laid on my mat with my classmates, with a few white children in my class as well, placing the puzzle pieces in the right places. Little Black Sambo, always shiny and bright, was supposed to be an image of me. I didn't know that at the time.

Incredibly, even the fun places had signs that said, "Whites Only," swimming pools, parks, recreational areas. There was only one swimming pool we could go to and it was far from our home. We could go to the park near our home. It was a lovely place with massive fir trees at the top, loaded with soft mulch beneath where pinecones made their home over time. The grass was beautiful, always cut, I suppose by the city. However, there were some pretty lovely homes across the street from the park. I bet they called city services to make sure the park was taken care of weekly. I think it was called Golden Hills Park. It only had a few swings, but they were maintained. We had to run up a very steep hill to get to the swings. We didn't mind though, because we always rolled down the hill to go home. Itchy, scratchy, but content, we made it down. Lying in the grass, we watched the lightening bugs (fireflies) glowing in the dark on those summer evenings. Sometimes, we caught them and put them in bottles or paper cups, whatever we had at the time. We made our own fun. So,

I assumed Mr. Jim Crow was a white man who didn't like colored people.

***

Our schools and neighborhoods were generally segregated. The grocery store was owned by a white family, as was the hardware store. The drug store had an Asian manager, whom I assumed was the owner. A small dental office and a photography store were owned by colored men. In fact, the dentist lived on our street and every year he drove a brand-new pink Cadillac. We loved to watch that car coming down the street, especially if we were playing our homemade game, "Choosing Cars." The premise of the simple game, that had to be quiet to please our father, was that every car that passed the house was given to each of us. We needed only to sit quietly and wait. Child by child, we waited our turn; and if it was your turn - - and if that pink Cadillac came past our house, you would win. Just like that! We shouted with glee for whoever won. We cut our exuberance short, if we heard our father yell from upstairs, "You kids, be quiet. I need my sleep. If you can't hear, you feel!"

Chapter 9

My mother asked her boss for a personal loan. It was for a down payment on a new home. My father did not want her to ask for the money, because he was a proud man; but finally, he agreed. By the time he could save enough money from his extra jobs, his family would be bursting at the seams.

Her employer gave my mother a handwritten check for a thousand dollars made out to the lender. My mother was anxious. She had never seen that much money before. How would she pay it back? But she was truly grateful! Her growing family would have a real home.

***

One of the ministers in the church we attended gave my father the connection for our last home on Rockwood. It was an unusual living arrangement. Our family lived with Mrs. Day in her home. Mrs. Day was probably in her late seventies I thought as a six-year old child, because she looked ancient to me. She had crumpled skin that looked like someone had crushed it in their hand like paper, or crushed velvet wrinkled fabric. Additionally, totally bedridden, Mrs. Day was completely blind.

Rightfully Hers

I didn't understand why she couldn't move her legs. They were right there on her bed with the rest of her body. I could see them beneath her bedspread. No one took them. She wasn't missing any parts like the men I saw in wheelchairs, who were injured in the war, they said. Her legs weren't broken either. So, what was wrong with them?

Then they said she was blind. But I could see her eyes. How could you be blind, if you had eyes? That didn't make any sense! How is it that she couldn't see? Why were people saying these things? Her eyes looked dark. The white parts weren't really bright. They were kind of yellow brown. I can't really describe it. But she had eyes. I know she did.

I made silly moves with my hands, face and legs, while in her room. Mrs. Day's room was always dark. I could not understand why that was necessary, because she couldn't see anyway. Her room seemed somber, bordering creepy, but clean. No odors in there! If I stood at the entrance to her room, she somehow knew I was there, but standing there gave me a good look at her room. Mrs. Day's room was actually the living room of the house, so the main entrance was a double door entrance with gold, tone on tone, damask fabric gathered on a wooden rod. There was a smaller door off to the side, where Pauline, her caretaker, kept the sheets, blankets and night gowns she used for Mrs. Day. It was probably a hall closet originally. The front picture windows had pleated blanket lined drapes in a heavy gold brocade. Her bed was a dark copper metal framed bed, with a footboard, that matched, simple yet sturdy, with Mrs. Day always under the wool blankets. Next to the bed, which was next to the wall, was a bedside table with a radio on top. On the shelf below the table was a small record player, where Pauline played Mrs. Days favorite tunes.

I was always checking to see if Mrs. Day was faking, watching her eyes for movements. I just didn't understand how a body could be affected in this way. I could actually see her legs and her eyes. Orlando said that she really couldn't walk or see. He said that the functions in her brain no longer worked, and that lying in bed so long, her muscles weren't any good. Atrophy was the word he used. I found this hard to believe, but Orlando knew a lot about so many things.

Another question was, how could she talk, if parts of her brain did not work? I only asked Orlando these questions. Norman stood next to me, inquisitive, yet serious, looking at Orlando too. I didn't want to bother the adults with my inquiries. They may have thought that my questions were rude, too invasive into Mrs. Day's life. Mrs. Day would say to me, "Come in Dear," with this comfortable, but high-pitched yet fragile voice; then she coughed, as if it took all her energy to greet me. She, somehow, always knew when I was standing at her door, no matter how quiet I tried to be.

Over the next two years, I got to know Mrs. Day and her caretaker, Pauline. She was really a sweet old lady and she didn't smell funny either.

I told you that Mrs. Day's bedroom was actually the living room of the house my father rented from her. The downstairs bathroom was hers, but we could use it in a pinch, if it was opened. Well actually, Mrs. Day could not use the bathroom. Pauline helped her with a bedpan. So, the downstairs bathroom was used only for getting rid of stuff and filling the small wash basin for Mrs. Day's twice daily birdbaths, which Pauline also took care of. Our family had the second-floor bathroom and three rooms upstairs. My mother and Pauline shared the cooking in the downstairs kitchen, which led to a large backyard with lots of grass.

I never understood why Pauline pulled the gathered curtains and closed the living room drapes. They were only open for maybe an hour. After all, if Mrs. Day couldn't see, what difference did it make? So, what if the sun came in!

My sister, Elaine, was born while we lived in Mrs. Day's home.

So now, there were five children.

A couple of years after we were living in our new home on 34th Street, my mother received a phone call from Pauline, Mrs. Day died. My mother was sad, and I was too.

***

No one else occupied the new house on 34th Street, but our family. So, this was really our first and only home - three bedrooms upstairs, a bathroom, and the living room, dining, kitchen and a service area on the entry level. It had a big grassy backyard, a cement pond which Orlando found filled with coal, dirt and ashes, and a small yard off the alley by the garage. It also had a large metal well in the backyard, with a big black heavy iron top. You had to be strong to lift it. When Orlando and his buddies raised the lid, the metal container had water about three quarters of the way down. Everything was black in that well, including the sides of the container. No evidence of light! I don't know how they got that humongous container in our back yard, and below the ground. It didn't appear that anything lived in it. We didn't have a long pole to agitate the bottom, for possible animal bones, or something else like human baby bones. My mind ran away with possibilities in that water. When we first got the house, there was a pump next to it, that Orlando dismantled.

***

During the summers in our new neighborhood, we took walks after dinner (a couple times a week) to the Dairy Queen (DQ) for strawberry malts and soft served ice cream cones dipped in chocolate. On Sunday evenings, sometimes our father gave our mother money for our treats. With that money, we ordered our specialties, Banana Splits with strawberry, chocolate and chunked pineapple syrup, crushed peanuts, whipped cream and a maraschino cherry on top.

This casual walk took us about a half an hour to get to the top of the hill, across the street from Crown Hill Cemetery. The sidewalk was initially okay, only a few broken areas at the beginning where the corner electric store did business.

During the days when I rode my bicycle all the way down that long block, I saw big commercial trucks run over those walkways, making deliveries.

Rightfully *Hers*

As we progressed up near the top of the hill, there was no concrete, only dirt and gravel with lots of dips, mud sometimes, if it rained.

I held my mother's hand and Eddie's. My mother held Elaine's hand. Norman ran ahead, kicking rocks and jumping or pretending he was running a race in his high-top tennis shoes. Many times, Orlando rode his bike with extra lights he put all over it. We could see his bike in the next block. It looked really neat. While waiting for us, he went to the bait shop next door.

My mother was comfortable on these walks. We talked and laughed at the comments my younger siblings made. We talked about the children she had at work. They were important to her. The night air was usually humid, and by the time we got to DQ at the top of the hill, we were hot and famished.

First, we stopped in the bait shop to get Orlando. We could see the front wheel of his bicycle leaning against the shabby, whitewashed wall with the kick stand down. The bait shop was a fascinating, yucky place. I was amazed at all the fishing lure you could buy there.

On our tippy toes, we hung over metal sink basins filled to the brim with earth worms, big fat ones, with lined textures on their tubular bodies. I don't know what they fed them, but they were huge. They also had another variety that were very long and thin, and they could jump out at you. There were also basins filled with crawdads trying desperately to get out, crawling over each other struggling to get to the top.

What I loved the most were the aquariums filled with little goldfish in various colors. Too many to count, and I tried! Orlando bought fish in plastic bags, which he hung from his bicycle handlebars, like the ones you get at the Indiana County Fair, but in little bags, as a prize.

***

Our neighbors on both sides were white. In fact, most of our neighbors were older white people. Only our neighbors to the right had children our ages who we played with, and their family owned the grocery store on the corner. However, the following year they moved. In fact, the majority of our neighbors moved away, and black families came in. Some were teachers, others owned businesses, worked in city government, bus drivers, factory workers and a number of them were retired. The exception was our neighbor to the left. I was a little frightened of him at first. I saw him stumbling around his front porch. My mother told me never to go to his house unless I was with Orlando. Our neighbor was an older white man, probably fifty years or so. He was an alcoholic. That's what Orlando said, and he sometimes went to his house to help him. His house matched his appearance. A few times, Orlando took Norman and me there, he looked messy and disheveled. In fact, his home could be on an episode of 'Hoarder." I did not know that people lived like that. We sat with him on the front porch which was loaded with old newspapers; but there were lawn chairs. We could not get into his house.

I could look into his living room picture window, or the glass winter frame of his screen door. Believe me, you could not see the floors. Liquor bottles, all shapes and sizes, some brown, clear, shiny, and newspapers old and new filled his house along with mail, thrown haphazardly over everything. Just like he decided years ago that he didn't like papers neatly stacked. No, he separated the sheets and threw them into the air, probably enjoying the experience of watching them float down. There may have been some furniture beneath, but you could not tell. It was clear that there was no place to walk. Norman and I stared, with our mouths opened, as we waited for Mr. Talbert to come to the door.

"You guys wanna' soda?"

We never accepted any drinks from Mr. Talbert. I was mesmerized with his face. Big mega marbles, Orlando called them Hoagies, and shooter marbles called Hickees were on both sides of his head. It looked like real marbles were beneath his taut and shiny skin. They weren't always in the same place. His hair trimmed, but stuck up in thin spikes, some flattened on the side where he probably slept on them and the other side sticking out like nails from his head. His face was shaved, yet a little wrinkled skin hung below his jawline. He had lots of missing teeth, however, he was always laughing and talking.

He would say, "Hey Orlando, can ya fix my ra-da-o fa me? I knocked it ova again."

He had a hard time articulating, because he had empty spaces in his mouth where he should have had teeth. Sometimes, spit came through the openings, especially when he laughed. So, I stayed back and just listened, trying to be pleasant. His clothing had a yucky sweet urine smell which blended with the jasmine vine on the lattice shade on the end of his porch next to our home. On his small framed body, with wrinkled arms and neck, boney chest, he usually wore a plaid cotton shirt and old gray trousers that looked like the bottoms to a suit. It was clear, he balled them up at night, because the wrinkles were so pronounced. He pulled his belt tightly at his narrow waist with an old wide leather belt, notches with big holes, with a brass buckle.

Orlando always treated him with respect. "How are you doing Mr. Talbert? Do you need any help today?" He liked that, and the fact that this teenager could actually fix things.

Maybe three years later, Mr. Talbert died. I wondered, did he die in the house, and it took them weeks to find him among all the debris. Luckily, it was winter. His body was probably frozen.

***

Years later, my mother showed me a receipt for the last payment on that thousand-dollar loan. She was very proud. A smile captured her face, and her eyes danced. She said to me as she held the paper in her fist, "I didn't know how I could do it, Beverley; but I knew God would find a way....'Ask and you will receive!'"

My mother asked God for many things in my life that I could remember, and He made things happen for her. If she had not asked her boss, we would never have had a home of our own.

I was proud too.

Chapter 10

Her warm tiny body felt like a soft puppy snuggled close to my leg. When I looked into her small bright almond eyes, her miniature yellow oval face was imbued in a smile. My mother said she wasn't planned, but she was certainly loved, and she was easy to love. Yvonne was child number six and she was truly delightful. Walking in three months and at six months she could run faster than baby hamsters scurrying from their cage.

Older women at church and some of our neighbors told my mother, "Daphne, you shouldn't let that child walk and run around so early. It will ruin her bones, and she's going to be bowlegged....

I didn't know if that was true. So, I checked Yvonne's legs, often, to see if there were any noticeable indicators that I could see.

Another friend of my mother said, "That child is going to get stepped on...She's too little to be on the floor...."

Well, she really was little, because she was so young. So, that was likely true. I kept my eye on her, so no one would step on her.

Rightfully *Hers*

Watching her was like watching a 'Tom Thumb' movie. She looked like a doll, so tiny and beautiful, in little dresses with ruffles standing at attention from stiff petticoats that our mother selected for her and starched.

I wondered what these nosy women expected my mother to do. Tie Yvonne up until she was a year and a half! Yvonne was however a happy child, rarely ever cried, always excited about the world around her. She was seemingly an older person in the body of a child with maturity and understanding far beyond the average scope of the child her age. By the age of two, Yvonne could read an entire series of Dr. Seuss books and by five years old, she was a prolific reader, easily mastering chapters of the Bible and local newspapers. She was truly remarkable and my mother's simple explanations for her gifted child were, "She's only trying to keep up with her older brothers and sister. She came here knowing that I didn't want any more babies."

Well a baby, my mother did not have.

Sometimes when I was out with my friends and took Yvonne along with us, strangers asked me, "Is she your daughter?"

"No," I replied, "she's not my daughter, she's my sister;" but I could easily have added, 'She's not my child, but she certainly has a great place in my heart.'

***

Yvonne was lying next to me on my mother's bed and listening as my mother read. She laid flat on her small protruding belly with knees bent up and legs swinging back-and-forth. Yvonne was wearing a bright red, cotton zip front romper short suit. She also wore white knee-high socks and red canvas shoes. I helped her dress every morning.

In fact, all of my mother's children were in the room that day listening to my mother's final chapter. We didn't know that at the time. We just assumed that she would go on writing. Somehow the second portion of her life must've been just as painful as the first, with the exception of the joy her children brought. Her life centered around a painfully staggering relationship with her own mother, and a relationship, void of affection and kindness, from her husband whom she often admitted with bittersweet remembrance had changed.

**

"Yes, life in America, it's never a bed of roses. You don't lie around and expect things to happen. Well, I am writing about myself. Maybe for others, it was a little different. Boy to me, it was like being born again!"

I saw "Life in America," written on the page of my mother's Murphy folder for seemingly a year, before I would again witness another single line written by her. I checked the folder periodically and I asked my mother if her story was finished. Her answer was always the same, "Oh, I'll get around to it," but she didn't. So now, one year later, I was anxious to hear my mother's simple, honest words leaping from a pure heart and determined spirit.

***

"Only this time, I have three of the most wonderful children God has ever given anyone. Yes three! Was everyone looking at me and saying, 'Dummy, where are you going with three children in America?' Unconsciously I'm saying, 'They are mine. God gave them to me, and He will take care of them and me;' because my husband was not ready for them. We didn't even get a hug at the airport. I tried to hug him, and he gave me a very nice push off. I was so glad to see him, but then I didn't have enough sense like I have now. You see this little epistle has taken me about 45 years to write. Funny in America, 'land of the free and Home of the brave,' my husband pushed me away from him.

Why was I here? I will never forget it! That's sad. There are many things I would love to forget, but I won't, until I leave this world!"

***

I felt a sharp pain in my stomach, reliving our arrival in America, feeling that there was definitely something wrong that day. My father was not happy to see my mother.

Now, my mother confirmed this situation again in her journal. When she walked up to my father, excited by their re-union, he had gently pushed her away. My mother had been startled by his behavior, but said nothing, allowing my father to finish passing out the coats, and to get re-acquainted with his children.

During the five years that my parents lived apart, my father had begged my mother to come and join him in America, but she would not, because she refused to leave her children behind with his parents. So, I guess my father was still angry with her. Yet I heard, actually I was eavesdropping years later, that he had met another woman, a white woman, someone from a church in a nearby county, which my parents had to reconcile. Rumor had it that the lady might have been pregnant, but I don't really know if that was true.

***

These words, "...*Until I leave this world,*" were written on white notebook paper, but as they floated on the wings of my mother's shallow breath, the words harvested a quiet anguish. I watched my mother figuratively step from the journal of her life's story, to the young girl my mother was then, again hiding in the folds of its pages.

My mother literally died a million deaths in the infusion of emotions that bound her tightly in swaddling clothes; but brought her neither warmth nor comfort. The first day she stepped on American soil with a daughter clinging to her skirt and two sons, anchored like marble bookends providing a familiar yet fragile support, she met the second major obstacle of her life. Rejection by her mother was the first. Now, rejection by her husband, the man she had chosen, because he had been kind to her.

This rejection pulled her inch by inch, as she struggled, into the abyss of the ocean that separated her from my father. I heard the faint melody, "Bless be the Tide that Binds," behind the deafening volumes of water dragging like sludge in and out to sea. Older people at church were always singing such songs during morning devotionals, yet I never quite understood its meaning. I watched my mother's face, as the words rustled forth from her lips, in and out, as the water joined the rhythm of the words.

I felt the icy-cold whitecaps of the Pacific Ocean rushing over my mother's weakened body as she stood in the icy mist of the deafening volumes. Winter temperatures of the water penetrated her warm golden yellow skin and sturdy bones. The consuming water burned the membranes of her nostrils and engulfed cavities foreign to her, signaling messages her brain was ill prepared to meet or change. Her lungs were singed from the mounting infernal of holding her breath and knowing the finality of letting go. Terror was growing within her like defiant water beating its back against a dam of indifference. Her eyes, bulging from pressure, incinerated by the salinity, joined its tears to the bellicose flood of unwelcome aggression.

The consumption was powerful, fast, complete. The struggle needless, useless, ...--Then nothing! ... Numbness, inoculation concluded! An angel, outstretched arms, stood as a beacon to her new home.

But it didn't happen that way! Only in my mind! Each time my mother prepared for her demise, and in turn laid a foundation of preparation for me regarding her early death, she was spared.

The angel was familiar to me, however. She visited me one night in my sleep, although I swear that I was very much awake. I went to bed early that evening after taking an antihistamine for a bad bout with cramps. During the night, I was visited by a beautiful lady in a flowing white nylon chiffon, floor length gown. Her long arms and slender hands were invitingly extended like a mother reaching for an injured child. My eyes were immediately drawn to the soft folds of her enchanting dress. The fabric was alive, moving fluidly like milk running across a glass table. It was heavenly whispers of clouds. There was a slow steady progression towards me, even though I could not see her legs.

From the mattress of my twin-size fold-a-way bed, I watched this stunning woman move elegantly towards me. When she reached my bed, she knelt. Caressingly, the fabric of her skirts, soft as the belly of an infant, brushed my arm like an artist's loving stroke on a canvas. I looked into a kind, gentle face. To my amazement, the image of my mother's face was mirrored affably into my own. I waited, perplexed. In confusion I whispered, "Mother?"

There was no recognition on the lady's part. Puzzled, I uttered again, "Mother," slightly louder this time, but still no response. I sensed something was strangely wrong. A crescendo of panic ushered through my small body, gradually taking control, drawing me in. My breath shortened and my heart quickened, pounding like bongo drums in my chest, and reverberating throughout my body.

I knew it was not my mother. The congenial expression on the woman's face metamorphosed before my eyes. Something ugly, grotesquely evil manifested itself into a representation of my mother. Now a phantom relished in the knowledge of this deception and my personal fear. The pounding in my chest became all consuming, deafening. I felt as if every part of my body was now 'a timpani of rhythmic pulsations.' I started to scream, when simultaneously the lady began to strangle me. The strong bones of her fleshy fingers dug into my moist skin, squeezing the muscles and tendons of my neck.

I tried desperately to scream again, "Help!" But it was as if I choked on a piece of meat. No sound came forth, just this maddening, magnified drumming pulse resounding throughout the canals of my ears, while my body became the sounding board of its magnification. Strangulation eminent and terror was paramount!

The soundless screams never left the raw dungeon of my throat. Muscles strained beyond their limits hopelessly struggled through concave walls of terror and lifelessly gave in to the unrelenting tension. I could feel and see the colors: red, warm blood pumping through my veins heating up like the

145

mounting pressure of a teapot over clinging flame. My hands tingled from the construction. In my head, vivid crimson was injected into ink spots of immutable darkness. 'Black, the color of my true love hair,' a song ran through my head, black the absence of color. Black, the absence of my life.

Submerged in this conversion of darkness, fear grabbed blindly, scraping the bloody surface of my mind. In my own voice I heard this declaration piping through my brain as clearly as music in the dentist office. 'You are going to kill yourself. You must relax. You are going to kill yourself!'

I gathered all my strength while systematically willing my mind to concentrate on the basic function of breathing. I took deep, full breaths, filling my lungs with air like helium tanks quickly inflating large balloons, as the piped in message continued. My heart was still a thunderous locomotive in my small chest, but I willed myself to focus on the motion of my breathing, simple, just coming and going. With each penetration, ebbing and flowing as the ocean breathes, I could feel the fingers of the phantom's boney hands, lift one by one from my thin neck.

Horrified, I stared in disbelief as the phantom rose, returning to the statuesque lady of classic charm and elegance. She walked gracefully with the long flowing, classical form of a ballerina, captured in the pupil of a hologram, … out of the room … out of my life.

Dripping in perspiration, I was petrified. Totally exhausted, I watched the apparition still visible in my mind.

Only my eyes had energy to move. In the moonlight, illuminating the room through the sheer drapes where the store-bought satins didn't quite meet, I saw my two younger sisters sleeping soundly in the full-sized bed across from me.

I searched frightfully into a callous darkness, fearful of ever closing my eyes again. I waited for what seemed like an eternity for the early morning sun to rise and my mother to come on her morning rounds of waking us kids.

***

The sound of my mother's voice was a precious gift, and one that I waited desperately for. It was gratefully received even though the giver had no idea of the extent to which that gift was needed. My mother's voice was the only other human articulation I heard since the desperate memory of my own voice, seemingly hours earlier. Anxious, I never left my bed. I could not, even if I wanted to, because my body was initially paralyzed. If I could move, I didn't know it. I waited apprehensively for my mother to complete the morning ritual.

I recounted the terrifying incident of the night to my mother. She listened, wanting to remove my fears. "It was a hallucination," she said with tears just on the rims of her own eyes. "You could've died in your sleep," she continued cautiously searching my eyes.

"I'm so glad that you had the strength to fight back. You saved your own life."

My mother asked me for the container with the remaining pills. She was going to talk to the pharmacist, a Chinese man, at the neighborhood drugstore where the pills were purchased. I believe that he was also the owner, because he was always there.

"You saved your own life," my mother repeated almost like a Psalm, but with fear edging in her voice. She seemed worried as if my experience had captured something raw within her. Perhaps, my near loss had been her own.

I heard my mother's words pitched forth from the darkness of that night. I clung to them like a life raft, "You saved your own life." I realized for the first time how close my walk with death was. As my brothers and sisters looked and listened in disbelief, my brain shivered in coldness. How someone could die in their sleep was now a permanent reference in the mind of a 15-year-old child.

Months later, my mother showed me an article in the Indianapolis Star. The antihistamine I had taken for menstrual cramps was removed from the over-the-counter medicines. Dangerous side effects were reported, which included hallucinations.

Chapter 11

"Well there were so many nights when I would lie down, I really wish that I was back in Jamaica. I found myself talking to God and I am sure at times when we were talking, he was answering because the next morning everything seemed okay. My problems had just begun, because this 'dumb broad' got pregnant again and had three more children: Eddie, Elaine and Yvonne. During this time, my husband and I, with the children, grow further apart.

***

It was clear from looking into my mother's defeated eyes that she had given up her dreams of a happy family life that included my father. She had grown up without a father and desperately wanted a father to be an integral part of her children's lives. My mother now 45 years old and my dad 52, she knew that he would not change. His actions made it clear that he wanted children only from a far. He thought children were too costly, and they stood in the way of the American dream he had for himself. The greatest problem his children presented, which he could not control and never openly said, was that we would grow up and start thinking independently, independent of him.

Our father really liked babies, though. He didn't mind getting up at night, giving them a bottle and rocking them to sleep. I have always been a light sleeper, so I was aware of night activities. He willingly and gingerly woke his younger children during the night, taking them to the bathroom or allowing them to squelch their thirst by cupping his large fleshy hands like an oversized cup for his toddlers to drink water from. He was different in the night with small children, a kinder gentler man.

I suppose it was because all his children were asleep, especially the larger ones, the house quiet, and all the utilities were off.

My father wasn't shouting, "Turn off the TV!... Turn off the lights....You're burning too much juice.... Stop running that water.... Don't walk on the carpet, you'll wear it out! Who turned up the heat?...Turn off that fan....You're wasting electricity! You're wasting water! You're wasting gas. You're wasting...." I knew the final line of our father's lament, even though he never voiced it, but I knew he thought it, "You Are Wasting My Own Life."

Strangely, he seemingly didn't care for children for which he was responsible beyond second or third grade. Just the presence of a larger body in the house added fury to his perception that children may at any moment step out of line, eat too much or use too much juice, as he called utilities. I thought that our cardinal sin against our father was simply that we would grow up, and in the natural order of things, consume more and in practice, disagree with his philosophy.

***

My mother referring to herself as a 'dumb broad' in her writings, I thought was strange. I hated it when she called herself that. After all, it was not an expression she normally used. It was 'common place' I thought, and it defined a woman through the eyes of a narrow man. My mother referred to her pregnancies in this common vernacular which was definitely an American expression. I heard this colloquialism on television comedy, radio stations, boys at school shouted, "Dumb Broad," to girls and laughed. I thought my mother believed this was a true reflection of who she was. I tried to contradict her, but there was something in her demeanor during her emotional lows, that said simply, 'The label fits.'

I read the "Scarlet Letter" in school; but my mother was married so this 'dumb broad' statement just didn't fit; but it was somehow as if females who didn't take the steps to prevent unwanted pregnancy or where women were totally dependent, men regarded them as 'dumb broads.' I never heard my father use that expression. It was definitely too American for him. His favorite expression was, "You're just plain stupid, man!"

Nevertheless, this expression didn't build self-esteem in my mother, only seemingly diminished it. But her instinct to protect and provide for her offspring saved her children from the emotional scars our father inflicted. Ironically, she could not save herself.

***

"Watch me Bev. I can jump from the top of the staircase landing to the floor," Norman boasted confidently.

"No, you can't! You better not do that, boy. You're just going to get hurt," I said.

"But I can Bev! Just watch me. Come on, turn around and watch me."

I paid no attention to Norman. Watching him was totally out of the question. Perhaps, he would just give up this fruitless challenge. I walked away, slowly making my way to the kitchen.

I could hear my brother's voice still pleading with me.

"Please Bevs, just look. It won't take but a second."

I ignored him. A brief silence followed, and I assumed that Norman had given up his idea, but then I heard him shout nice and loud, "OK, here I go!"

Nervously, I listened. Hearing nothing, I continued piddling around in the kitchen, just waiting in anticipation for his jump. I wasn't comfortable with the idea that Norman might actually do it. I don't know why, but I thought, he might just try. He looked so determined. We were supposed to look out for each other. Still, I waited and heard nothing. Then suddenly startled by what sounded like a suitcase thrown vehemently against the stairwell, I heard the deafening cry, "Beverley Ann," then nothing.

With my heart hammering in my chest and thrashing it in my ears, I ran to the foot of the stairwell. I saw my brother lying face down on the multicolored striped carpet. His legs were spread eagle in his Safari Bermuda shorts. His right high-top tennis shoe, with his foot still in it, was dangling between the white posts of the stairwell banister.

Like stones, neither of us moved. I wasn't even conscious of my own body. I just stared at his lifeless one, frightened beyond belief. My mind engulfed in maddening quiet. I just waited. I didn't know if I should run and call our mother; but then I would have to leave Norman alone. The wait seemed like an eternity. Then as if robotic, Norman raised his handsome gingerbread face, inch by inch, and then stared blindly into my own eyes.

From loss of breath and certainly shattered hopes, a weakened voice rolled forward on Norman's tongue. He barely spoke between labored breaths, "Help, help me," he said.

A moment of deadly stillness lingered between us. Locked in gripping fear, we dared not move. Silence prevailed. Our eyes embraced until, a smile slowly covered Norman's face like the sun recovering from an eclipse. We burst into laughter, tears running down our faces. I scrambled to pull Norman's right foot out of his laced tennis shoe, and the sneaker dropped to the hallway floor below, making a loud hollow thump as it hit the floor.

I smiled to myself as I remember that day, because my brother was okay. Today, there was no evidence of his fall. It is only a childhood memory in the minds of two children. It was Norman's first attempt at that distance, and he survived to make many more successful jumps after that day. I even joined him on a few.

My mother had fallen as well that first biting-cold day in December when she stepped on American soil and was rejected by my father. She used the words from the Star-Spangled Banner, "land of the free and home of the brave," to describe her feelings, perhaps a subtle reminder that freedom has never come without cost, without pain, or sadly, without loss.

***

I looked into my mother's weary eyes bearing the caustic agony of that first day in America and now recorded in indelible ink on the pages before her, as well as those in her mind. That message, like re-runs of old 'tear-jerker' movies, "Until I leave this world." The words mounted on the Statue of Liberty flashed through my mind. "Give me your tired, your poor, your huddled masses yearning to breathe free. ...Send these, the homeless, tempest tossed to me...."

***

The feathered pillows flattened immediately when I laid my head against the white ironed, pillowcases, which I pressed. I spent two to three hours ironing clothes in the basement. The clothes, dampened and rolled into balls, were stacked in a large, covered basket to keep the moisture in. I was always so relieved to get to the bottom. That summer afternoon, my dark brown eyes again focused on my mother sitting on the edge of her king-sized bed. She read again from a collection of handwritten papers entitled, "My Life's Story." The pages, bound in red gum backing, rested comfortably in her lap, as a metal window fan belted cool air into her bedroom.

***

I looked from where I was sitting to see my other sister, 'My Roy Rogers,' leaning against the doorway. She was smiling demurely, the fifth of my mother's six children. Elaine called herself, 'My Roy Rogers,' because she was crazy about Roy Rogers whom we watched on television every Saturday after my father left for one of his jobs.

She loved this cowboy character so much, along with his wife Dale Evans, Trigger, his horse and sidekick Pat, that she called herself, "My Roy Rogers." Everyday Elaine wore leather Buster Brown cowboy boots, machine stitched with colorful flowers, leaves and animals; a cowgirl hat, long sleeved shirt; and 'tough as a stallion' blue jeans with a zipper front and matching jacket. She was true to Roy's spirit: kind, willing to help and loyal. She never gave me any trouble. Elaine was gentle with a quick wit. She could find humor in anything. She had a quick comedic comeback for our older brothers' teases and jokes.

As a toddler, Elaine wanted Orlando to do everything for her. He played with her and carried her around. She would cry when he left, so Orlando found creative ways to sneak out of the house, so that Elaine would not be upset.

She walked in and sat on the wall to wall carpeting, her legs crossed Indian style. Her eyes had a playfulness about them, but she remained quiet. I looked at her and smiled. She smiled back. She was five years younger than me.

My mother's eye connected with hers as well. A raised eyebrow, just as Norman would do, acknowledged her presence.

My mother looked at all her children gathered in the room. One by one she studied our faces. She seemed surprised to see us all.

***

In the fifties, none of my friends ever shared that their mothers wrote during their free (not really) time, but their personal time. But my mother did, and I thought that was great. She wrote her story down, so we could read it, just like all the books she read to us as children. This writing, however, was really to pacify that lonely child within her. I wanted to listen and support my mother through this painful time in her life. My siblings were there for the same reason, I suppose. The younger ones, mostly enjoying the sound of our mother's voice. We all just wanted to be near her. I knew Orlando was anxious to go, but I was surprised that he actually waited. His buddies were now, just an after-thought. Just as our mother read to us from the nursery rhyme books when we were small, she continued to read to us. This past time, we enjoyed.

***

On other occasions when Norman and I were re-reading sections of my mother's journal when our mother was at work, 'My Roy Rogers' would come into the room.

Norman said, "What are you doing here?"

"I don't want you!" she stated sarcastically while giggling.

"Well, get out of here, you big head brat," Norman continued.

"I don't have to. Mother said I don't have to," Elaine snapped back.

"Well, Mother ain't here," he growled.

"Okay, okay, I just wanted to ask Bev, if it was okay for me to play with Jeanie," Elaine said quickly.

I nodded in agreement.

"I don't think so," Norman said in a slow roar in ascending octaves. "Because, I AM GOING to HUFF and PUFF...."

Elaine didn't wait for Norman to finish. She turned with the speed of lightening, laughing as she dashed down the stairs. I could hear her Buster Brown cowboy boots hitting the kick plates of the stairs. Norman followed behind, never fast enough to catch her, just enough to enjoy the chase for an afternoon diversion.

I put the binder away, just where my mother hid it between her papers in the headboard cabinet. I am not sure if she was hiding her story from us or from our father. Afterall, he was the one who had changed. Nevertheless, she would never be the wiser, I thought.

At the bottom of the steps, I could hear Eddie's voice. He joined Elaine, laughing at the top of their lungs with Norman. No doubt the big bad wolf caught up with 'My Roy Rogers.'

Chapter 12

During the two months of summer, when I was ten or eleven, I took care of my three younger siblings. Orlando was supposed to be around to help me, but he was with his buddies. In fact, in the mornings, I could hear his friends whistle a loud high-pitched sound, for Orlando. The whistle meant that they were to meet in the parking lot adjacent to the corner drugstore. Norman was running with his little sidekick, so generally, it was me at home with the children. With Yvonne in her crib, asleep, I planned activities for Eddie and Elaine. The stairwell became my classroom.

The front of the stairs, where I stood, was my imaginary teacher's desk. Sometimes, I moved the piano bench for my actual desk. I seated my students by height. Eddie on the fifth step, four years younger than me and Elaine, five years younger, on the third step. This is where I taught them mostly, music and drama, as well as read stories to them. I made up plays in which both children had parts. On occasion, I would make costumes for them, particularly if I felt their performance was good enough for our mother to see after dinner. Sometimes, my friend Betty came over to help me.

I kept a flattened, folded newspaper nearby in case the kids got out of line. I gave them a swat on their behinds, if they needed a reminder of who was in charge. But generally, they were well behaved.

Orlando came home for lunch and helped me fix food for the little ones, or sometimes he brought home hostess Twinkies or Hostess Snow Balls and Ding Dongs with a quart of whole milk, none of that skim milk stuff. While the toddlers gladly ate, and giggled listening to Orlando entertaining them with 'Knock Knock' jokes and Yo-yo tricks, I fed Yvonne rice cereal from a glass baby bottle and Gerber baby food in little jars from the grocery store.

Sometimes, the little ones wanted some of Yvonne's food like the fruits particularly. So, I fed them plums and apples which they loved. Other times, Norman and I would eat the plums too. Delicious!

If Yvonne wasn't well, my mother took her to work with her. It was then my mother's employer told her to bring Yvonne to work every day with her. After that, I only had to take care of Eddie and 'My Roy Rogers.' After lunch we watched cartoons, then around 2:00, they had a nap or quiet time, while I vacuumed and cleaned the house, a job I loved to do.

At 3:00, I would start their baths. When my mother got home after 5:00, the children were dressed in clean pressed coordinated outfits. When my mother walked in the house, the aroma from whatever she told Orlando to prepare for dinner invited her in. He always beat her home. Generally, he seasoned the food before he left in the mornings and put it in the refrigerator, or at times, my mother would do that before she left for work. Either way, the dinner was always tasty.

I had about a month with the little ones at our home during the summer. The other month was spent at my mother's work, when the family was in Europe. This was a special time for us, because we never saw so much space, both in the house and on the grounds, belonging to one family.

After breakfast, Orlando was picked up by Henry, one of the ground-workers, to work on other properties the family owned. He was payed for this summer job. Yvonne in the crib, Norman playing with 'My Roy Rogers' and Eddie, I was given little jobs like cleaning out the drawers, there were many, in the laundry room and Butler's pantry. Sometimes, I washed napkins in the washing machine, with my mother's help and ironed them along with table linens. Another time, I stitched the hems of the burlap curtains in the Sunroom.

To be honest, I didn't do a good job. I was flying through the fabric on an old Singer sewing machine, peddling as fast as I could with my feet, not taking my time. I probably should have pressed the seams in place or based them with white thread to keep the fabric in position; but I didn't. I was just trying to go fast so I could play with Norman and the toddlers. Like I said, I didn't do a good job, so my mother had to remove all the threads that were crooked.

Ironically, my mother didn't scold me; but I could see the disappointment in her face, as she removed all of my stitches. I had only done the first two sets of panels well.

Needless to say, the Sunroom was lined with windows, and there was plenty of work to do. I assured my mother that I would do a better job, and I could. I felt badly that through my negligence, my mother had to pull stitches from the panels, on a job that was simple for me to do.

Other times, I took every book off the shelves in the library to dust the books and shelves. Norman helped with this tiresome task. We did the cleaning section by section. Everything had a place. But I particularly enjoyed vacuuming and there were so many huge vintage Oriental rugs. I used an early forties Hoover upright vacuum with powerful suction in the massive hallway, huge living room and dining room, and a canister vacuum, with many attachments, in the sunroom.

After lunch, Norman and I could run and play on the property. We played tennis, ping pong, croquet and Marco Polo in the swimming pool, which was hard to do, because of the depth. We were constantly jumping up to avoid the change in depth, and then of course, we came up with mouths full of water.

Nevertheless, summers were lots of fun. Later when I was fourteen and Norman fifteen, my mother allowed us to drive her car back and forth around the mansion's gigantic horseshoe driveway, probably a fourth of a mile. We took turns and loved it! We were the masters of our destiny. The best gift yet! We were very careful, always staying on the paved asphalt, never veering off the road into the flower beds and grasses. We could never have done this on a city street; but this was a large private driveway on private property. By the way, we never told my father that we were driving our mother's car that he paid insurance for. Why should we? He would have been so mad, he would see fumes, I'm sure. My father would probably drag Norman and me to juvenile hall to tell the judge that we stole the car. Anything to get back at my mother for permitting such indiscretion! My parents would have argued about this adventure. The simple truth was that this opportunity would not exist, if our father knew.

Our time at the mansion was very special, and in Norman's mind and my own, that time cannot be surpassed. It was our favorite pastime adventure.

Chapter 13

I am thankful to God that I am not a lazy person, and I was told soon after I got here, I had to find myself a job. I did and I would have done anything just for peace and quietness. It is still a mystery how much my husband has changed. You never really know anyone on this earth. I guess not even yourself, because I surprise myself sometimes. It doesn't matter how anyone is, keep your eye on them always. You never know when they are going to go through the changing period.

***

I can remember arguments my parents had where my father, would pompously state, "Many are called, but few are chosen," taken from Matthew 22:14. He definitely believed that he was among the chosen for the work of Christianity. He truly believed that he could direct your path. I didn't think at the time that our father possessed the compassion or patience needed to be truly effective.

But maybe that wasn't true! Maybe, it was about us. We were the ones who didn't fit in with my father. Maybe, he could have been quite effective in another environment, with another family.

Whenever he started with, "Many are called, but few are chosen," my mother would shout back at him, "Remember Norman, you are the one chosen, Not Me."

My father would pleadingly say to my mother, "Daphne, you must be sensible (which he said all the time) about these things." My father, using his Sunday school approach, tried to draw my mother in, without the discussion turning into a full argument. It never worked.

My mother would repeat, "Just remember what I said, NORMAN, YOU are the one chosen, NOT ME. God chose you, NOT ME!"

My father, angry, would walk off in brisk strides.

Norman, my father, was quite astute at seeing all of our shortcomings, and we had plenty, but never his own. He made Orlando feel inadequate, hitting him with a ruler on his knuckles whenever he didn't answer problems correctly. Orlando had to endure endless comparisons to other young men: Play basketball like Tom -----. Go to Butler University like -----. Orlando hated reminders of our father's work ethics. "A man must work by the sweat of his brow. On that he will be judged… You see the pattern I've set for you." This was taken from Genesis, but of course, my father made it about himself.

Our father worked from sun up to sun down. He did not believe in pleasure. Pleasure, he said, was a waste of time, mere foolishness. We also hated his arrogance. He believed himself superior. His words were the only words that mattered.

He said Norman wasn't his son, because he was too dark, although he was the spitting image of his father, our grandfather. He refused to leave book money or school lunch money for him. My mother waited until he went to sleep, to settle the score. She made sure that Norman always had his money first.

My father's trousers hung or were mostly thrown up and over the top of the white door opening to their bedroom. It was easily illuminated by the hallway light, where Norman and I stood nervously watching our mother. 'What if my father woke up?' I thought, there would be a BIG argument. Oddly, he never did. With my father sound asleep, my mother removed money from his leather wallet in his back pocket. She gave the money to Norman, placing it in his hand. Each time, Norman smiled, put the money in his pants pocket, with a big look of satisfaction, then ran swiftly and quietly down the stairwell with his bow legs.

I wondered how Norman coped with the meanness of our father. No, this was cruelty, based on ignorance. Norman willingly accepted this handout, that our father did not want him to have. This happened every week for his lunch money, unless my mother noticed that there was more than what was usually there. The cost of lunch was $2.50 per week, fifty cents a day. But somehow, Norman did not let this arrangement bother him. He went on with a cheery disposition. I would not have handled this well.

I waited for my mother to put our father's wallet and pants back in its original place. On one occasion, I asked her, "Why does Daddy do that? It just doesn't make any sense. Norman never did anything to him. He is the only one of us kids who looks like our grandfather."

My mother regarded me. I could sense her anger as well as her hurt. She was haggard by this knowledge, weighted down by my father's ignorance. She took a breath, then said, "If your Daddy thinks he can deny one of his own children by his skin color, he's sorely mistaken. Cha, he's got another thing coming." Then she moved abruptly and turned away from me.

I could see her breathing heavily in the light coming only from the hallway. Moisture sprinkled across her forehead. I looked at my father peacefully sleeping. He never knew we were there, and we did this every week, usually Sundays. My father was way too tired from his fulltime job and his two part-time ones.

I was perplexed by my father's behavior, his thinking, his cruelty. I thought he was a religious fanatic. However, he went to work every day, two to three jobs, provided for his family, and always took care of himself. He was a good worker. He saw himself as brilliant, the rest of us as sorely lacking.

Our father was a Christian man, thoroughly devoted to his calling and beliefs; but the reality was that – he was human, with human frailties and human shortcomings.

On the weekends, I heard numerous speeches that my father recorded on his reel to reel tape recorder. His accent was so strong that even I had trouble understanding him. He sounded like a foreigner; but I guess we all were. My father, however, loved to hear his voice on that audio equipment, and he would listen for what seemed like hours to his voice. We were, however, not allowed to touch this machine.

Chapter 14

My mother never wrote again in her journal. I saw her write countless cards to friends and family, receive letters from her mother Phyllis, to which she always replied. She sent all her children and grandchildren, cards and gifts for all special occasions.

My mother continued to be a beacon in our lives, and that of our children. Long before my mother's death in 1988, when her health was fragile, my daughter Mia insisted on calling her after an incident in San Diego. We spent a few days on Mission Bay, which we loved to do during Easter Break.

The Mission Beach Boardwalk, with its shops, amusement park and ocean activity, was crowded with people, wall to wall, enjoying an afternoon out. It is a great place for kids. Mia, about eight years old, and I were walking and talking, hand in hand, when a bicyclist ran right into Mia. Mia fell and was so angry. The bicyclist and the bike fell too. He barely said, "Sorry." He was in such a hurry. He jumped back on his bike and took off. Mia's hands and knees were bruised. We stopped at a near-by Lifeguard first aid station to clean Mia up and applied antiseptic to her wounds. As Mia and I continued walking awkwardly, my arms around her shoulders, and Mia's arms around my waist, Mia said that she wanted to call her grandmother.

"I have to tell Grandmother what that man did to me. He just ran into me, just like that. Like he didn't see me...." Mia said whimpering.

"Okay, Sweetpea," I said trying to cheer Mia up. "When we get to the hotel, you can call your grandmother."

At the hotel, Mia couldn't wait to tell her grandmother all the details of her accident. After talking to her, she felt so much better. Her bruises would take time to heal, but emotionally, Mia was better. My mother could always make you feel better. It was a gift she had.

My daughter, Mia, and my mother were very close. When Mia needed an advocate to support her point of view, I would get a phone call or letter from my mother saying, "I think it is time that Mia gets an increase in her allowance....Mia really wants that Irish lap harp, etc. I don't see anything wrong with Mia having a dog." All the subtle reminders of their talks and communications. Their relationship was special. I liked that.

My mother continued to buy my daughter's school clothes for the beginning of each year, just as she did for all of her children. Even when I was in college, my mother still bought me clothes for the new year. I loved receiving those gifts. It was exciting looking at the new fall clothing lines, while checking to see what would look well on me. The clothing was expensive, and I wondered how she paid for them. But a gift is a gift, and I accepted the clothing with the full measure of kindness and endearment given.

My mother sent me cards and letters all the time, because I lived in California. She celebrated many weddings, anniversaries, deaths of friends and family, divorces of her own children and friends, while she struggled to support her children, those well and ill, and grandchildren. She was there for her friend Elmore. Following a horrific car accident, Elmore's infant daughter and husband were killed.

Orlando, my oldest brother, was in his twenties, and I was a junior in college, when he was hit while getting out of his car by drag racers. His duplex was off Northwestern, a transition road to Interstate 65, a beltway that looped around Indianapolis. He was in the hospital for almost a year.

I awoke early that Sunday morning after Orlando's accident, with strange feelings I did not understand. I called Clarence, my boyfriend, at the rental house he shared with two other roommates and asked him to please drive me home.

Clarence, immediately sensing something from my voice, said, "Is there anything wrong?"

"I don't know," was my reply. "But something tells me, 'I have to go home.'"

Luckily, Clarence didn't have to work in the campus cafeteria that day, and he said that he would be there shortly. He picked me up in his 1953 mint and forest green Buick. He bought the car from an elderly white couple in Muncie, Indiana for $175.00, during his third year of college. This couple was the only owners of that vehicle. The husband said to Clarence, "Take good care of my car, young man."

Clarence, happy to own his wheels, said with a giant grin, "I will Sir." He paid the owner in cash. Accepted the keys and drove off.

The car was definitely vintage, but it hadn't been restored. You could see tiny pockmarks on the chrome in need of repair. It had, however, a good motor and drove well.

Clarence looked 'out of step' with his fraternity brothers who drove newer model cars like the popular 1963 Pontiacs and Fords, but he was not in competition with them. He was confident in his own person. One of his buddies had a 1968 Ford Galaxy. His roommate drove a 1962 Chevrolet Impala, which he paid for with his fulltime night job at a factory in Anderson, Indiana. Well, Clarence was not driving a new car, but at least he had a car, and did not have to bum rides off of his buddies.

We were en route to Indianapolis, and I still had that odd feeling. Clarence said, "What do you think it could be?"

Again, I said, "I don't know. But something is definitely wrong at home."

After an early morning lazy two-hour drive, we arrived in front of my childhood home at about 9:30 am and got out of the car. I saw my mother at the door. My mother smiled a tired grin. Now, I knew that something was definitely wrong, just looking in her pale, drawn face.

I said, "What is it? What happened?"

"I didn't want to bother you, Beverley," my mother said sadly. "You have schoolwork and so much going on in your life."

I looked into her kind face and spoke gently, "Just tell me," I said now feeling real panic.

My mother shared what she knew about Orlando's accident. Clarence and I listened.

That afternoon, we went to visit Orlando in the hospital. We had to wait until the 1:00 visiting hour. He was so happy to see me and Clarence. I was definitely surprised to see him.

The corner room was stark white, and the afternoon sun shone brightly through the petite striped cotton pleated curtains. A single brown imitation leather chair with wooden legs was adjacent to the bed in front of the windows. Shiny linoleum tiles in tic tac toe patterns and a restroom completed the space, although my brother had to use a chrome silver potty pan, because of his leg.

The rest of the room was taken over by metal, probably polished chrome, apparatuses attached to his bedframe. Pulleys and angular poles extended above my brother's body. You would have thought this was a gymnastics room. However, my eyes could not leave the image of Orlando's leg dangling about two feet above his body with a highly polished silver nail protruding through his ankle.

Each time I tried to focus on what my brother was saying, I found myself staring at the polished silver nail probably about five inches long going through his foot.

The skin on half of his face was gone, removed by friction burns, down to his shoulder on the same side which matched his half face. A salve covered this part of his face and shoulder. I could not imagine that Orlando may have to be bed bound like this for almost a year. The doctor said that his leg that sustained the major impact would have to be re-broken surgically after the swelling went down. Orlando told us what happened that day.

"When I got out of the driver's seat of my car, before I knew it, I was flying through the air, man. The initial hit was to my right leg, that's where those rascals hit me. That blow sent me soaring through the air, like I was a beach ball." Orlando laughed and then looked in wonderment.

"I came down on my shoulder on the sidewalk in the next block, can you believe that? Then I slid on to my face. The doctor told me that if my body wasn't so built up from playing football in high school, I would have broken my neck. That's wild man!" He moved his head slowly from side to side, a bewilderment in his eyes and repeated, "That's wild!"

I pictured the incident as he spoke. The next block was a good walk from his home. Orlando had a thick neck and his upper torso matched this thickness. He was stocky, and the bulk saved his life. I imagined those guys going so fast, that their car propelled his body into the next block, and probably didn't know they hit him or didn't care. They probably said, 'It's an accident, man! I didn't mean to do it.' Unbelievable!

Orlando was not angry though. He was his usual 'happy-go-lucky,' self. Believing that his survival was all that mattered. Having raced cars, a future member of the Corvette Club of America, he probably had no hard feelings about the guys who hit him either.

I don't recall any conversation about the perpetrators. We were focused on Orlando's recovery. They got away clean!

With my mother, there were other numerous health challenges, injuries for family and friends as well. Nevertheless, 'life goes on.'

***

Four of us went on to get college degrees. I went to Ball State University on a music scholarship and in my final year, I was selected for "Who's Who in America." Eddie went to Virginia Common Wealth University on an athletic scholarship but was injured. He later completed his undergraduate degree at Ball State University. Yvonne graduated Cum Laude from Indiana University. Elaine went into technology after completing her degree. We all began professional careers. Norman went to the Navy earlier and later joined the police force and became a detective. Orlando survived his year in the hospital with nurses fussing over him and bringing his favorite foods. He moved on to automotive mechanic repair, for which he had received top honors at the Indiana state competition in high school. Ironically, he still enjoyed racing and was a member of the Corvette Club of America. Later, he drove big rigs for a brewery company, but still struggled with injuries from that accident.

***

I met my husband Clarence in the Student Union building (the Tally Ho) of Ball State University Muncie, Indiana, in September of 1965. The school was a teacher's college at that time. We both were freshman and wanted to be teachers. Clarence, particularly, because he was told by his high school counselor that he would never make it to college, along with others in the neighborhood who believed poor children could not succeed. Clarence was determined that he would. He went to college on an athletic scholarship in track and later became a nationally ranked Athletic coach. Growing up poor, but in a loving family of ten children, with a father who worked and came home to his family every day, Clarence succeeded, as his mother and father knew he would.

***

Grandchildren, now abound, with bachelor's degrees, masters' degrees and law degrees, and many other accomplishments and challenges. My mother's social security check helped make it possible to support her grandchildren in a meaningful way. By the way, all the years mother worked as a domestic in the mansion, her employer paid into social security for her. Commendable!!

She was there for her employer when their son was killed in Vietnam and their daughter en route back to her home. She loved these children like her own.

In the 1960's, my mother decided that she would send for her mother, Phyllis, the one who left her emotionally depleted all her life. She was concerned that her mother did not have health care in Jamaica. At least here in America, you didn't die without medical support.

My father supported my mother's decision and paid for my grandmother's ticket; but he did not want Phyllis to live with us. There was not enough room anyway, but I believed that he had enough of Phyllis when he was a young man dating my mother.

My grandmother, Phyllis, lived in Indianapolis in the next block with friends of our family for three to four years. Later, she moved to California with Clarence and me in Altadena. Altadena is a small city nestled at the foot of the San Gabriel Mountains and Eaton Canyon. We were at the foot of the mountain, not far from Jet Propulsion Laboratory (JPL), which manages NASA's Space Network.

My grandmother came to help me with my pregnancy and was a big help to me initially. When we came home from work, dinner was prepared, home cleaned, and Phyllis even picked flowers from the yard for the table. But there was definitely something amiss! She made statements like, "Young people shouldn't live with old people," and a number of times, she would not eat with Clarence and me, saying, "You need time for yourselves."

***

Clarence had many of my mother's qualities and understood life struggles as a black boy growing up in the ghetto. He and my mother were close. The two of them were always laughing and joking.

He and my grandmother, Phyllis, got along well too. Clarence is one of those people who gets along with everyone.

***

Then later, when I am fully into my pregnancy, my grandmother moved to her own apartment in Compton, California, with the encouragement of church friends. It was there, five years later, that she became a victim of a violent crime.

During her recovery, she lived with my family again, but we now lived in Los Angeles. Clarence got very ill from Altadena's beautiful environment, with horses, chickens and tree distributing pollens. His allergies could not handle it. He developed acute bronchitis, which led to trouble breathing. The resulting cough was dreadfully painful. His doctor advised that this city was not for him. Our family moved back to Los Angeles, in the community we first lived in when we arrived 1969, before our baby was born in 1972.

My grandmother was comfortable in her new apartment, although her health was a concern, until the day a man knocked on her door. He said that he was selling papers. My grandmother told him, "No know you Sir, and I do not wish to be troubled or disturbed by you...." This is when the man kicked opened the door, and Phyllis became a crime statistic. Without coaxing from the family, she went to court to confront her assailant and won her court case.

My grandmother, Phyllis, took no pride in her win, and said, "Me couldn't help me-self though, Mistress Bevs; couldn't a'tall. Him too strong, but me could help somebody else, see Miss Bevs? You see the circle supporting life? Me could help somebody else. Me proud for that! Yes, me proud for that..."

We were quite proud of her too. After her recuperation, she rented an apartment a few street blocks from us, which made it easier for Clarence and me to help her.

***

After the death of Phyllis in 1987, ten years after the crime, Daphne struggled with her own health, both emotionally and physically. We established a doctor for my mother when she came to visit Los Angeles. She had congestive heart failure with fluids building up in her lungs. Rather than taking her completely off salt, her doctor suggested salt substitutes. She said that many of her patients who were completely off salt, lost their appetite, then had no desire to eat, which lead to further deterioration.

***

My mother and father continued to drift apart. My father never really understanding her health concerns, or did not choose to, because she was younger than him. His pointless argument was, "But she is seven years younger than me...." Needless to say, that had nothing to do with her health. My father didn't seem so brilliant to me, then. Nor when he telephoned me in Los Angeles, because as he said, "Beverley, I just found your mother on the floor wedged between the bed and the wall. Your mother is not breathing."

After catching my breath, I said to him angrily, "Get off this phone right now and call 911. Do you hear me!" and then I slammed the phone down. Strangely, I thought, my father could only remember my phone number and I lived the furthest away. Three of my siblings lived right there in Indiana, and he called me, the child he had argued with all his life.

The paramedics came to our home and administered insulin to my mother and gave her orange juice. It turned out she was in a diabetic coma. She lived for many years after that incident.

My father was clueless about health and illness. He, like so many people who are not accustomed to being caregivers, just don't get it!

***

So, my mother's writing just sat there in the buffet drawer – a location she later moved her book binder to - believing that she could just pull it out one day and continue writing. She didn't even have to change clothes. Easily accessible!

I believe that my mother's disappointment in marriage added to her emotional state. My father, she had chosen; but later questioned her choice. Her mother, she had no input.

Chapter 15

I stood in the dining room of my childhood home in November of 1988, everything looked the same, like a picture in time. I stood next to the telephone bench, which once sparkled with Pledge Furniture Polish, adjacent to the white built-in corner cabinet. There was nothing different about the cabinet, other than some of the glassware and platters needed washing. Then I picked up the white Princess phone, the latest model with the dial, mouthpiece and hearing mechanism in one area on the top. The base had only a cord protruding from the side attached to the top. I looked at the airplane tickets that I held in my other hand.

For some reason, I was distracted, but couldn't understand why. The young lady, from the airlines, repeated, "Ms. Clarkson, the date is in the upper right-hand corner. Do, you see it there? Ms. Clarkson, can you hear me? We must have a bad connection," she continued.

I was lost, something in me just took over. I felt an overwhelmingly strange sensation each time I looked at the date, but didn't understand why. I could feel an energy pumping through my system, hitting at the walls of my senses. My forehead felt moist, and I was spent; but shouldn't have been. Just anxious! Still staring at the tickets in my hand, I tried to continue the conversation with the ticket agent, but without success.

When I tried to voice the date again to the employee, I was once again captured by this strange feeling. This wonder took over my mind, my heart, my body. I felt a rumbling in my brain, like signals were getting crossed, confusion strangling my thoughts. My mind became an echocardiogram, but the sound waves were jammed, and this reflected in my consciousness as a moving picture recorded on paper. I took a deep breath, steadied myself. While looking at the plate of Queen Elizabeth sitting on the cabinet shelf, the date finally came out of my mouth. I held the tickets in my hand, still not understanding what was happening to me.

"Ms. Clarkson, we must have a bad connection," I heard the employee repeat.

Finally, able to confirm our plane tickets - dates, time, etc., with the airlines, I hung up, looked at the tickets a little suspiciously – still not able to satisfy what happened to me. I opened my purse, then placed them inside.

"We're all set," I said to my mother with a big smile, shaking off the strange feelings from the moment before. I didn't talk to her about these feelings. My back was to her, so she was clueless as to my stress. I didn't understand what was happening to me anyway. The tickets were confirmed and that was what mattered.

My mother looked up at me from the dining table. She was so happy to be home from the hospital. A smile overtook her face. "I never thought that I would make it back here," she said with a slight hesitation, as she slowly eyed the room around her. "I thought your father didn't want me to come home."

I thought about what my mother said, but my father seemed genuinely happy to see her home, when we came through the front door the evening before. He literally, lit up!

The old man standing before me, straightened his shoulders, seemingly adding two inches to his height.

"You home now?" my father said with a big grin!

"Yes," my mother said; but I could sense her anger.

"I will be leaving for California with Beverley," my mother responded curtly.

My father continued, as if he hadn't detected the provocation in her voice. "That will be good. The weather is better out there, anyway. Give yourself time to relax and recuperate."

***

A couple of hours before, while waiting in her hospital room, my mother was very anxious. "They are not going to let me go," she continued.

"Yes, they will, and we have a plan for your care. They will not keep you here against your will."

When the nurses came in with the wheelchair, my mother was now convinced.

"We're going home," I said with a smile.

Daphne turned to look at me and immediately relaxed, a softness embraced her face, and she beamed, and thanked the hospital staff for their support of her health. My mother was always a gracious woman.

I walked along side my mother as a staff member pushed her wheelchair to the patient pick-up area. My sister Yvonne, working in Human Resources, met us there.

My mother struggled with congestive heart failure, fluids building up in her lungs and body tissue, for a number of years. It was progressively getting worse.

The following evening, my brothers and sisters came to my parent's home after work, along with spouses and children. The house was full of laughter again.

I watched my father with his hazel eyes, a little glassy, shoulders slightly rounded now, his back tilting towards the floor. There was no evidence of the physique and stature he had as a young man, and the meanness he personified in me as a child.

He beamed as he unhurriedly advanced the stairs to escape our boisterous gathering. He was happy to see us all there, but we were too much for him. It's not like you can tell grown children to be quiet.

I knew my nieces and nephews well, because they came to California and spent a number of summers with Clarence and me. They were everywhere, having their own little pow wow. Orlando was, however, the life of the party. He had us literally in stitches.

He was a natural storyteller and his experiences were so unusual, no one could compete with him. So, I just sat back and enjoyed myself, laughing until tears filled my eyes. Actually, my siblings could hold their own in the humor department. Yvonne and Elaine were also quick wits.

It felt good to be home, and to see our mother enjoying our time together.

***

It was comforting, the next day for me to see my mother tending to her business, wearing a house dress her mother, Phyllis, bought her on one of her trips to California.

My grandmother, with a big smile, told her, "I want to buy something nice for you, eh? Me just take you to one of the little shops in the neighborhood me go to."

"Makes no difference to me," my mother said a little chafe.

Phyllis, my grandmother, appearing somewhat anxious continued, "Cha, me just want to give you something nice from me. Just a little something!" Then, she grinned.

So, I took my mother and grandmother to the small shop, where my mother selected a dress; subsequently with Grandmother's encouragement, she selected two more dresses, a red Moo Moo (Hawaiian pattern) and a Maxi, which looked quite nice on her.

It was one of the three long dresses, my mother was wearing – the polyester one with a black background, with small colorful flowers printed all over. This one had long sleeves with cuffs, zipper front and two attached fabric ties at the neckline which could be tied into a large ribbon, or draped down the front, covering the zipper.

My mother sat working at the hostess end of the dining room table, where my father always ate his breakfast, alone. She was getting papers in order. I looked over at my father's desk in the front corner of the dining room, and it was its usual sloppy mess; but no one ever bothered it, and he seemed to know where everything was. Only on special occasions did my mother stack his papers and letters neatly. I even did that a few times.

The dining room had wallpaper on the top half of the walls. There were two different patterns I remembered over the years, that my mother selected and paid a professional to lay. It was a large comfortable room. It had chair rail moldings around the room, painted white as the lower half of the room was painted, including all the base boards and wood trim around the doors and the built-in corner cabinet.

The room's paper was currently a mint green and white swirl pattern. On the front-facing wall in the center of the room was a large beveled edge mirror with a five-foot mahogany buffet server beneath. The server matched the large table with leaves in it to seat our family. The entrance to the room had large wooden pocket doors, which we never used. As a child, I thought the large pocket doors made the dining room look haunted. With floor to ceiling draperies pulled to each side by matching fabric ties, no one knew that the pocket doors were there.

The exception in that room was my father's desk. The piece that didn't fit in, just like the life my father lived with his family. He was the absent-minded professor.

Chapter 16

Six days later, we were leaving for Los Angeles. It was early morning. My mother walked slowly down the stairwell of our house on West 34th Street, my childhood home. She was the "Queen for a Day" we watched on John Masterson's television show. The only apparel missing was the robe and of course, the crown. My mother spent the last month in the hospital.

***

While she was in the hospital, we talked briefly on the phone each day, she in Indiana and I in Los Angeles. She told me that she did not want to die in the hospital, and no one would sign her out. She felt trapped. I promised her that would not happen. I would come to get her. She said, "Bev, you're the only one who would do that for me."

To fulfill that promise, I took a personal leave from my work as an Assistant Principal. I figured it would take me a week to bring my mother home with me, where she visited me each summer and had recuperated many times before.

I talked with my best friend, Alice, at the time, whom I met my second year of teaching. She was a history teacher, and like me, was now an Assistant Principal in a high school. She was quite fond of my mother from Daphne's many visits. She laughed and joked with her, as did all my friends, enjoying her accent, which I never noticed, unless my husband or friends asked me to tell them what my mother said. I also shared my plans with my high school principal. Like Clarence and me, they believed in my decision to support my mother's wishes.

***

That morning, my mother's movements were like that of a model, eyes bright, looking straight ahead. Her brown eyes connected with those of her grown children, the ones my mother never thought she would live to see grow up. She looked fabulous, in her full-length pastel mink coat with her initials embroidered in mauve threads in the inside, matching the lining, a must have! The coat was certainly befitting the Indiana winters, and her fur hat.

My father looked up from the entryway hall below when he saw her coming down the stairs, his eyes bright and said, "Well, Well," with a luminous smile. My mother returned a shy 'happy face' smile. You would have thought this was one of their courting dates, with my grandmother Phyllis hiding vicariously in the background, hostile to the young man taking her daughter out. They both seemed genuinely pleased to see each other.

Norman's hazel eyes, like a deer in headlights, were gleaming while his body stood motionless in a red and brown plaid flannel pajama. Shoulders slightly hunched over; but I thought his heart that morning was that of a much younger man, possibly the one who said to my mother, "You are a lily in a stagnant pool, and I'm going to take you right out of it…."

Yes, I believe that was the man standing in the entry hall of our home that day. The one I longed to meet. The kind man, the gentle one in my mother's writings, the one I wished I met in childhood, not at age forty-one. It was actually him that morning. I didn't talk to him; but acknowledged his presence with a nod and he, likewise.

I saw this man first in the pupils of my mother's reflective eyes and then in the old man that stood in the entry hall below, in pajamas, waiting to say 'good bye' to her. He knew that she was comfortable in California, and even though my mother actually liked the Indiana winters, I knew the weather in Los Angeles reminded her of Jamaica.

***

I never hugged my father before we left, because that was not the kind of relationship we ever had, nor did I discuss with him my mother's pending fears. I don't know if my mother shared with him her thoughts.

***

In fact, the first time I remember being in my father's arms was years later. He held me as we danced at Clarence's and my 25th Wedding Anniversary. It was strangely odd; but as we danced in the midst of well- wishers, friends and family, in a lovely venue with fresh flowers abound, I followed expected decorum. My father, I remember, was elated. He was a different man when he did not have to pay for our lives. Less hostile!

I was nervous dancing with my father. After all, we were estranged my entire life. I could never dance with him in our childhood home, because he did not allow music in the house that involved the touching of bodies. He would have considered that decadent, crass by his standards. It was only when he went to work that we played rock 'n' roll music on the stereo my mother bought. In fact, my mother moved our father's full-size Hammond radio to the basement and replace it with this modern stereo system. On that Hammond radio, we could hear all sorts of languages from faraway places. Sometimes, it was China, other times Russia, as we played with the knobs on the set. Strange, really, yet interesting!

But on the stereo, you only heard the records you played. It was a five feet wooden furniture cabinet, a part of the living room decor. It had two doors that opened in the front with light brown mesh material behind them for the speakers.

Sometimes, Orlando turned the speakers up full blast, so loud, that the room and furniture would vibrate. Norman and I, laughing hardily, covered our ears with both hands, screaming, but no sound came out. I could see Orlando laughing too, but I could not hear him. On top and center of the cabinet was the record player hidden by a lift top that matched the rest of the mahogany chest.

Now that I think about it, I bet my father never knew it was a stereo, or for that matter, even knew what a stereo was, because he didn't pay attention to such things. My father only sat in his burgundy velvet chair, the one that was too big for our house, in the living room on Saturday nights to watch his favorite, boxing matches: Rocky Marciano, Sugar Ray Robinson, Joe Lewis and Sonny Liston.

Orlando bought every record that came out, from his pocket money earnings fixing cars. We danced with our friends and our mother in the living room and watched American Band stand on television. When we watched Elvis Presley on the Ed Sullivan shows Sunday nights, my mother was with us. My father was generally sound asleep on Sunday evenings and if by chance he awakened and came down the steps, he never challenged our mother in front of us kids. My mother would not stand for that. My father, on the other hand, only listened to religious or classical music. No exceptions!

I didn't know that my father could even dance or would want to dance. My mother did say the two of them danced all evening at their wedding. I never knew the man who held my mother in his arms on their wedding day. Yet decades later, here I stood in my father's arms, uneasy. I had mixed feelings. It felt odd, like I was dancing with a man I did not know.

Norman, my father, was five feet eight inches tall, muscular with big shoulders and biceps. His hands, large and corpulent, were warm, soft and comfortable. I felt the heat on my back from his ample arms circling my small framed body, guiding me, tender, gentle like I was his little girl. The child he carried from the airport when I first arrived in Indiana was again in his arms. He was a confident dancer, light on his feet, like the boxer that he trained to be. This time, I did not tug with him for the lead, as I did the day of my wedding. I smiled instead, relaxed and allowed my father to have the spotlight he craved.

As a little girl, I can remember the feel of my father's large fleshy hands while holding my little hand in a brisk walk to wherever we were going. He was always in a hurry. I'm sure to get away from us, but he had to drag me along for some reason. It didn't happen often, but I can remember the feel of his hands. They were much softer than my mother's hands. He never had the miserable, workhorse, childhood my mother had. His family looked up to him. They were so proud of him. He was their hope for a brighter future.

I am sometimes reminded of Luther Vandross' song, "Dance with My Father," and his longing to relive that experience. Well, I did get that chance once in my life, as an adult.

*** *

My mother continued majestically down the stairs, her eyes shifting from her children to her husband, probably remembering the man whom she said changed. She reminded me to keep watching. "You never really know anyone on this earth. I guess not even yourself, because I surprise myself sometimes. It doesn't matter how anyone is, keep your eye on them always. You never know when they are going through the changing period."

Had he returned? Was it this morning, seeing my mother's dark brown eyes glowing, well dressed, as he was accustomed to, not lying in a hospital bed angry with him over words never expressed between them? Was this the day he returned, the day he slipped in quietly beyond the gray consuming Indiana sky? Did this morning remind him of that lily and his promise to my mother?

I sensed an intimacy between my parents. One I had not seen in a number of years. It was communicated through their eyes. My mother's confidence was restored, and her continence embraced that morning. Validated by my father, the one she had been watching.

No one would have known from looking at her, that days before, Daphne had been in a hospital bed for a month in a dry wash soft gown, feeling like a hostage. In fact, she told me that she believed her stay was extended, because my father did not want her to come home until she was well. That's what they all wanted. My mother knew, however, that she would not get well, and felt she was running out of time to get her affairs in order.

It was odd to me what she wanted to take care of: clothes to the cleaners; sheets washed and folded from the dryer; her mink coat, which I paid the monthly bill for and she now owned, and other furs that she wanted me to have – her mouton lamb coat my father bought for her in the late 1950's as a Christmas present. My mother always opened her gift from my father at midnight. I remember her opening the large package. Her eyes were screaming with joy, as boundless tissue paper and ribbons fell to the floor. My mother was breathless. It was a flare coat with a lined collar that could cover the ears. It was quite heavy.

I helped her move other coats, each in a zipper-lined cotton bag to her suitcases. I felt there was no reason for this, because I lived in California, where it is rarely cold, and certainly not cold enough to wear mink or mouton, other than for show. Well occasionally, it might be!

She spent the first days at home, paying bills and writing letters to friends, and calling her dearest friends. She had a lot of catching up to do. That made sense to me.

"You were the only one willing to come and get me," she repeated. "I didn't want to die in that hospital bed, in that drab gown." I thought about my mother's years as a struggling pauper child wearing gunny sacks for dresses, crusted bottom feet, and no shoes. That experience diminished her spirits, ravished her skin and being. She didn't deserve that again in her life. So yes, I understood her need.

**

Later that same day, the family gathered around my mother at the airport to say their final goodbyes. In the background, I saw my father. He probably drove himself to the airport, alone, something he preferred doing, never really enjoying the company of family members in his car. Too many, perhaps, or we might say something out of line with his perspectives! He looked hopeful. Happy that our mother was going to a place she enjoyed.

Rightfully *Hers*

My father stood like a tree, steadfast, but he could bend, twist and sway whichever way the wind blew. He would be alright. His face radiated confidence, a belief in the faith of my mother. I knew he could stand alone at this time. It was something he had always done, stood alone. Never really a part of his family! Never the father who cheered boisterously for his children in the stands or in the auditorium. He was the father who didn't attend our activities, most of which he thought were foolish, child's play. He could not participate in such activities. He was busy with life as he shaped it, and as he worked by the 'sweat of his brow' to produce.

He did, however, like that I played viola in the school orchestra, because he bought me my own instrument when I was in the fifth grade. And later paid for music lessons. I was one of maybe two students who had their own instrument. The majority of the children paid a rental fee to the school for the instruments they played. I still have that instrument. He never came to any of my concerts though, he probably thought they were too immature. Not really concerts, just practice sessions in front of an audience! Not cultured enough for his taste.

There were only two events I recall my father attending on my behalf- my high school graduation and college commencement. Of course, he attended my wedding and paid for it, as the two of us tugged with the directions going down the aisle.

I wanted to walk down the center of the aisle, after all, it was my day. My father wanted us to share the walkway. He was paying, I suppose. He paid for everything including my

197

dress. My dress was just beautiful. It was A-line, flattering to my thin body at the time, with a lace overlay and the patterns on the lace were embellished with pearls not expensive ones, but small faux pearl beads. My uncle, my father's brother, sent me as a wedding gift, my first cultured pearl necklace. The back of my dress had a built-in train, with pearls added to the back as well, complimenting the front. For the reception, I needed only to pull up the train, with the help of my attendant, to the attached hooks.

My father was so proud, when he saw my dress. He quickly wrote a check for the purchase, and he was all smiles. I couldn't believe it at the time. He paid the bill for everything I wanted (within reason of course). My older brother's weddings were not to my father's liking. They did not give him the fanfare he wanted. So, he was glad to make my wedding special.

My father and I tugged at each other on my wedding day, as we did all my life, but this day was supposed to be 'My Day.' I don't think my guests noticed our tug of war, because we were both smiling, as we walked the long aisle to the sanctuary, presenting the appropriate faces. When I asked Clarence if he noticed my tug of war with my father that day, he said he didn't notice. However, Clarence did have a Bachelor party the night before.

***

At the airport, my father Norman watched his children encircle his wife, Daphne the lily, giving her love, comfort, prayers and praises. I believe he was satisfied that he plucked a lily from stagnant water and saved her for a better life of joy, with children surrounding her who loved her.

As each child, now grown, stepped back from my mother that morning, I, alone, walked with our mother on to the plane. The lily, my mother, stood firm, upright and stunning. She was able to go the path alone, before becoming too fragile and succumbing to nature. Just for that, my father was grateful, swelling inside with pride, as he took deep breaths with an internal sigh.

At that time, security measures at the airport were not strict; so, we could sit in the lobby and wave to departing flights or wait for incoming passengers. And if the plane left for departure in the right direction, you could see the small images of your family members in the lobby standing behind the plate glass windows. I saw the miniature of our family waving and was comforted by that view, and I knew my mother was too.

Once on the plane, my mother slept initially. When she woke, she talked about things that were on her mind. She said that it was important to her to get all her things in order, things she could not do in a hospital bed. But one thing she shared was that my father told her the night before that he wanted her home. He said he went along with the children's advice to keep her in the hospital until she was better, but it was not what he wanted. My mother knew she would not get better. She needed to come home.

My mother smiled puzzlingly, deep in thought, as she uttered, "All that time, I'm wondering why he didn't come and get me. Thinking, he didn't want me to come home. I'm questioning, what kind of marriage do I have, where my husband would not come and get me? I really didn't understand!"

Hearing my father's retiring conversation, the night before, brought my mother much satisfaction, as she settled her life physically and emotionally.

Following breakfast on the plane, my mother and I talked about a number of things. It was important for her to share her feelings. I was a good listener as I had always been. She prepared me again for the last time. She spoke softly, like she didn't want to scare me or be a bother, "Beverley, I will be dead before the end of the week." Her voice louder than a whisper, but words clearly articulated. I didn't respond, just smiled and touched her arm softly. Her mink coat which she used to keep warm, rested comfortably on her narrow shoulders. Her illness had taken the girth from her body. Even though, she was seemingly strong, her body was thin. My mother was quite ill.

But here my mother was again preparing me for her death. Now my mind jumped back to that conversation in my home I had with her, because my mother always thought she was going to die.

**

I remembered the conversation vividly, I had with Mother when I was in my late twenties. My daughter was about three years old at the time. My mother always spent a month with me at my home and at my sister's home during the summers, when I had time off before the new school year started.

"Mother, why did you tell me all my life that you were going to die?"

We were eating breakfast at the small bistro table for two in my dining room. Clarence and I often ate breakfast there, because it was more intimate than the two of us sitting at the large dining table for eight. The small round table was in front of four panels of vintage French paned windows. I placed a small centerpiece of handpicked flowers from the yard on that table. My mother looked up from her bacon and egg breakfast. Her whole demeanor changed, and she looked sad, truly remorseful.

"Beverley," she said. "I really thought that I would not live to see any of you grow up…. But you did! All of you did." Her eyes were glossy, and her forehead shined from perspiration.

"I am sorry I placed that burden on you as a child. I don't know what else to say. I am so sorry." She grabbed my hands and squeeze them.

I knew she was sorry. It was something she was somehow compelled to do. She had to tell someone, and that person was me. I knew it must have been really hard to live with such gripping thoughts. 'Thinking you were going to die!' 'That death was imminent!' 'That you didn't have much time!'

And then you did. I wondered what time was lost to my mother with such consuming thoughts. What did it take from her?

We looked into each other's eyes and smiled. This woman, my gentle mother, would never deliberately hurt me.

***

Here we were again, I'm 41 years old, and my mother is now sixty-six! Yet again, we smiled at each other, and squeezed hands. Mother dozed off into a gentle sleep. I was reading a book seated next to her on the plane.

I had an aisle seat and my mother had the middle seat. When she awakened, she said that she had to go to the restroom. I got up, waited in the aisle until she passed me and followed her to the lavatory.

My mother walked confidently and proudly towards the front of the plane. There was no trace of the illness that betrayed her over the past year. Just before she opened the restroom door, she turned around and smiled at me, an easy comfortable smile, and I smiled back. She looked brave and confident of where she was going. She opened the door and closed it behind her.

***

I remembered my grandmother Phyllis telling me the year before. "Mistress Bevs," her voice was weak, but clear. She paused to take another breath, then said softly, "Miss Bevs, I won't be here next week. You understand? Eh, Miss Bevs?"

And she wasn't! I recalled how devastated my mother was by her death. After Phyllis' service, my mother was sitting at my dining room table, consumed in pain. Between perforated sobs, my mother uttered, "She never once told me she loved me."

I've read about the connection between heart health and emotional health, but there hasn't been enough research on the subject. A mother's detachment from her child, can cause distress, leading to heart disease. My mother carried the pain of this detachment for a lifetime, even when she actually lived with her mother, Phyllis, she knew she was not wanted. No doubt she was drowning in her own fluids(congestive heart failure),for Phyllis, the mother who never wanted her as a child. At least, I believe, that is how my mother felt.

***

Standing outside the restroom cubicle waiting for my mother, I heard what sounded like her bracelet hit the floor. Then the sound of something heavier slumped against the door. I knew instinctively that my mother was gone. I reached for the door handle, but the door was locked. 'Occupied' flashed at me in red letters, backdrop in white light.

I stood my ground, feeling that I was now a guardian for my mother, and waited for the flight attendants to help me. No one would knock on that door and disturb her. This was my mother's time, and she was beginning her transition.

For the landing, ironically a seat was available for me just behind the restroom. I am not sure if the attendants moved passengers; but I was able to stand there as people passed to disembark. I was the last passenger on the plane, when a number of security and staff members boarded, quickly unlocking the facility, lifting my mother's slender body, covering it with a white starched sheet, and the red airline blanket, then placing her body on a gurney.

We exited the plane through this cavernous baggage collection area. I followed behind the gurney, walking proudly, carrying the red plane blanket given to me earlier by the Attendant, my mother's mink coat and the miniature Bible. I had never been in this section of the airport. In an office, I was able to call Clarence, my brothers and sisters, and a funeral home to transport my mother's body.

It seemed like a lifetime, but Clarence came to pick me up. He had to be directed to this area. Eyes red, his heart broken and matching mine. He didn't say a word, just hugged me, as I collapsed into his arms, and our tears joined in memory of my mother.

I wasn't afraid for my mother. I knew she was well prepared for her final journey, and this time she would go it alone. Orlando, Norman and I holding on to her skirt would not be with her, not this time; nor would her last three children, Eddie, Elaine and Yvonne born here in America. For her final journey, she would be alone. No earthly reminders of her family.

She would be embraced by a higher power. One who had been looking out for her over a lifetime. Each time she said, "I just want to die," and prepared me for her death, He had other plans for my mother. Now she would see Uncle Harold, Grandam, her father, her first-born child, and yes, she would see Phyllis, and this time my grandmother would be so excited to see her. Yes, she would grab her and tell her that she loved her.

Well, that is what I wanted to think, but I'm not so sure. But at least Uncle Harold, bringing her hot crossed buns from his bakery and Grandam, her great grandmother with loving and caring embraces, would take good care of her; and she would hear Grandam tell her in that cherished voice once again, "God bless you, my child."

By the way, Uncle Harold (really her Great Uncle) remained a source of cherished love for my mother over the years. She often mentioned Uncle Harold, tall and lanky, yet kind and endearing, with a captivating smile encompassing his gentle face. Uncle Harold lived to be 86 years old, and even though my mother no longer wrote to him, she kept him alive in her heart. I realized it was essential for her to do that. He provided my mother with that fragile balance between love and hate.

We smiled when we talked about him. It was as if I knew him. I could see him in my mind's eye, towering above the crowd, with his tall self, rushing towards my mother as a little girl, long and thin, yet muscular arms extended carrying hot buns from his bakery. I also imagined him sitting with Little Daphne in his white sharkskin suit, and Panama straw hat encouraging her to make the best of a bad situation. I saw the grin on my mother's face when her uncle encouraged her to do her best in school, and he was proud when she passed up her cousins in school. We actually laughed when we talked about all the children he had fathered by different mothers, never married, but he found time to make them all feel special; and even took a liking to my mother, finding time for her too. He still holds a special place in my heart as well, because he was one of the few family members who actually loved my mother.

***

My mother said in her writings, "Funny in America, 'Land of the free and home of the brave,' my husband pushed me away from him. Why was I here? I'll never forget it. That's sad. There are so many other things I'd love to forget, but I won't until I leave this world."

I somehow felt confident that my father, just by telling Daphne he wanted her to be home, brought my mother unbelievable satisfaction. He was not pushing her away this time. The first time she had nowhere to go, but to follow him with their children. This time, my mother had options. His words made her final homegoing one she could leave without regret. BECAUSE THIS TIME, he, my father, Norman Elston, wanted her with him.

Chapter 17

I think back on that day sometimes. Glad that I was walking with my mother, sharing our last time together, her last time on earth. Even in death, my mother was proud. She had reconciled the pain of her childhood. She probably would have written in her journal 'Daphne still searching and seeking new adventures.' As she crossed into the next realm, she didn't need me to accompany her. However, since she spent a lifetime preparing me for her death, it was my honor to walk with her that last time.

Needless to say, the passengers on our flight were delayed; but they were nice to me. Strangers exchanged smiles with me or touched my shoulder as they left. One lady handed me a small red bible, with a page folded back that she wanted me to read later. Another lady gave me a miniature "New Good Bible" on a keychain. The airline attendant folded the red wool-blend blanket, which shrouded my mother in death and handed it to me, after her body was removed from the plane. I felt like I was at a military event, being bestowed with an American flag.

A world wind of activities took place. Luckily, my mother had all her medications with her as well as a primary care doctor she visited here in Los Angeles. Therefore, we did not have to have an autopsy to determine the cause of death. In Indiana where her funeral would be held, my siblings handled all the arrangements.

Yvonne, a member of the cemetery board, handled the legal matters. Elaine worked with my siblings on the program, including the obituary. Eddie in his profession handled the flowers and communications. Norman and Orlando made the transportation arrangements for family and close friends, and the food. My girlfriends from Los Angeles paid for the funeral tribute bouquet on top of the casket. My mother, years before, selected what she was going to wear. It was a soft pink nylon negligée that Norman gave her as a Birthday gift. My father made the arrangement at the church where he was assistant minister. I prepared and read the Family Tribute for my mother.

Clarence, my daughter Mia and my niece Jean, Orlando's daughter, whom Clarence and I raised were sitting with me. I could feel my daughter's slim fingers on my back and shoulders, as she tried to comfort me.

Clarence joined me on the podium for gentle support.

These were the words I read at her service in 1988.

To Mother

With All our Love

From the time we were children, my mother shared with my brothers, sisters and me the humbling, painful experience of her childhood. Painted vividly on the canvas of my mother's heart were pictures of a thin, leggy girl in a burlap drawstring dress, barefoot, always waiting and hoping. The gentle child never had a sense of family, never truly belonged, but was determined to have a better life.

She didn't know at the time that she was part of God's master plan. He saw in her a gentle kindness, a charitable heart, a simple honesty, a loving spirit, an inviting sense of humor, a spiritual sense of being, an unwavering pride, and a staunch determination. She fit the prescription he needed. He wanted only to prepare her for a unique assignment. She needed a special strength. Through a menagerie of humbling experiences, he would prepare this child.

Rather than a childhood of happiness, hers would be one of suffering. Rather than a womanhood of trivia, hers was one of substance and quality. Rather than a ripe old age of just playing with grandchildren, hers was one of illness. He knew, however, that this poor little girl would someday be rich.

At each stage of her adult life when she reached her lowest ebb, God rewarded her with jewels. Yes, six semi—precious stones. Each one rare, reflecting life in a myriad of expressions, talents and gifts. The angle at which the light hit each gem was different. The colors of each one uniquely blended all the hues of the rainbow. Those jewels were her children. It was his will that she would take charge of us, keep us safe and love us.

The diamond, Orlando: caring, sensitive, dependable, talented with motors. The sapphire, Norman: charismatic, popular, gift of investigation. The emerald, Elaine: intuitive, sensitive, thought provoking, computer whiz. The pearl, Eddie: introspective, articulate, athletic, brilliant mind. The ruby, Yvonne: cheerful, sanguine, challenging, energized, organizational wiz. The opal, Beverley: dedicated, tolerant, compassionate, musically talented.

Our mother boasted of our brilliance, even though it required years of polishing and cleaning on her part to maintain our sparkle. Over the years, the trials and joys of our own lives dulled our surfaces from time to time, but the brilliance always returned, because it was the reflection of our mother.

We reflected our mother's ethereal glow, her sparkling eyes, warm smile and hardy laugh. We reflected her caring ways, her love for people, and her willingness to help. Each of her jewels were gifts of my father, a man she didn't understand, but respected and loved.

God made sure his caretaker was not lonely by enriching her life with the love of close friends like Aunt Phyllis, Rene, Elmore, Cletus, Joyce, Billie, Rev. Sanders, to name a few, and supporting neighbors like Mrs. Moore, Mrs. Potter, Mrs. Poindexter, Mrs. Johnson, and Ms. Carpenter.

Then to make sure that she had all the riches he wanted her to have, an extended family was added, the Browns, and the children she loved: Mary, DeWitt, Wendy, Judy and Carol. As her children matured, significant others (spouses) were added: Betty-Jo, Joanie, Rita, Clarence, Lori, Bob and Harold. My mother loved each of them like her own children. Added to this treasure was the loving addition of grandchildren and great grandchildren.

In our life time, all of us received from my mother the gifts she wanted us to have. The gifts were expensive, and she sacrificed for us to have them; but she lived by the standards and examples she set for herself. She said, "I'll give you flowers in life, not in death." Everything she did, she shared with us. We will cherish the memories of all those caring times.

She juggled limited time and money to take us on outings. Trips to the movies, shopping, lunch at Grant's with all the chicken you can eat for $1.29, basketball games, symphony concerts, swimming at Broad Ripple Park, ballet performances.

I laugh to myself as I recall my mother entering radio contests on who could scream the loudest on the telephone. At the top of her lungs, she screamed into the telephone receiver at 6:30 in the mornings; and she would win tickets. We sat with her at movies. I was really scared of course, watching Frankenstein, Werewolf, and Dracula.

She read stories to us and we laughed. Our hearts danced as the colorful characters came alive, creating within us excitement, sustaining in us, her love.

The little skinny kid, wearing a potato sack frock and barefoot, grew up to be, through God's blessings, the best dressed woman around. She dressed with the subtle elegance of a queen and on the other hand, the exciting flare of a fashion model, walking tall and proud.

All the years of my life, I remember my mother crying, because she felt so deeply. Tears were for her a sweet release. As each teardrop mounted and cascaded into oblivion, my mother would reach into her pocket. She always had Kleenex in it, dried her eyes and picked herself up.

Many of her feelings, she wrote down. I can remember lying on her bed reading chapters of her life story. She often read and listened to my stories, as well, finding delight, feeling and solace in them.

From the time I was a child, my mother prepared me for her death. She never believed that she would live to see her children grow up. She had always anticipated a premature death; but God knew better. She had to take care of her jewels. In the last month of my mother's life, she asked two things of me. First, she wanted to leave the hospital; she had to go home. Secondly, she wanted to return to Los Angeles, the place she had always gone to recuperate.

There were many parallels surrounding her departure on Sunday, November 6. She left Indianapolis in the heart of a pending winter, just as she had arrived in the winter of 1950.

For some reason, my mother's first-born daughter, Beverley, was chosen to accompany her on her final journey. My mother's first child, a girl, never survived her journey into this world.

My mother told me that she wanted to look her best. Her weak, frail body was adorned by her full-length mink coat, a new sparkling white hat, with scarf and earrings given to her by Lori, whom she loved as a daughter.

She was happy. She'd gathered her strength and awakened early that morning to get ready for her trip. Ironically, she was going home.

On the flight, my mother and I talked, and she shared her pain and her joy. She questioned why God had allowed her to suffer so. She never believed she would live the week. But she said, "Everything will be alright." She made peace with herself. She was comfortable and ate breakfast, which is something she never did on a plane. She said, "I knew of all my children, that you would come and get me." She thanked me for taking her to Los Angeles.

In the end, God was her jeweler; and He told her that He had gems she had never seen. They were more rare, brilliant and colorful than any on earth, and He needed a trusted, experience and valued caretaker. She fit the prescription.

My father always said, "Anyone who doesn't like your mother isn't worth a grain of salt," and you know, he was right!

Mother, we love you!"

***

At the end of the service, referred to as the 'Celebration of Life,' the minister asked members of the church to help by taking the floral bouquets outdoors. Immediately, people walked to the front, led by ushers, and carried out the flowers.

The funeral director with the Pall Bearers carrying the casket led, followed by the minister, then my father and our family. The procession continued. People stood in respect with smiles and tears matching my own. I walked with Clarence and my daughter Mia, my niece following with cousins.

When I crossed the threshold of the church's double doors, with tear saturated eyes, I looked into the brilliant sunlight to witness an unforgettable sight - a sea of flowers lining the walkway all the way to the street. I was overwhelmed. It took my breath away.

The child who was never noticed, never acknowledged, never even answered when she asked a question, was validated this day.

My mother always said, "I will give you your flowers in life." But I never dreamed she'd have all these flowers in death - breathtakingly beautiful!

Cultivated flowers of all varieties, some simple, like daisies, baby's breath, and sun flowers, others exotic like you would find in the bushes and countryside of Jamaica, Birds of Paradise, orchids of all colors including Phalaenopsis, Stargazer and white Lilies, roses of artificial productions (You would never find that color in your yard.), Calla lilies, red Gladiolas which I always have on my coffee table. All had been tended by loving, caring hands. That is what my mother should have had all her life.

The sun was bright, and the brightness embraced us with such joy. The weather was warm. My mother would enjoy this day, even though it was not a typical winter day in Indiana. Really, it wasn't. It was our Mother's Day, her homegoing, with the sun smiling down on her, family, friends and neighbors. I realized that my mother didn't need her mink coat after all. Good thing I left it in California. I was reminded in one of my grandmother's letters when I was in junior high school, the comment she made about my mother's mink coats and pieces. "Tell your Mama, I am borrowing her mink scarf to go to a party next week. 'Laugh!'"

***

I know you are wondering how a Jamaican family, even though we grew up in America, called Daphne, Mother. This is certainly not a Caribbean greeting. After all, we called our father, Daw-di, which is what most Americans call Daddy. Well Orlando, Norman and I decided to call Daphne, 'Mother," just like the Brown children called their mother, very American, yes.

We made a deal to change this familiar address. Each time we wanted to get our mother's attention, we were to use the agreed upon new change, "Mother." If for any reason we forgot, reverted back to our original name, "Mommy," the other two siblings were allowed to pinch you. You bet, we remembered!

***

I realized the day my mother died, with airplane staff seemingly running around me, the message that was intended for me. I held the plane tickets in my hands from our trip. The date flashed boldly before my eyes again, **November 6, 1988**.

My heart started pumping through my veins. My body heated up quickly, I could feel moisture under my arms, on my back, my forehead.

There before me was again the data I had been given on Tuesday of that week, but I didn't understand its meaning at the time. I guess my mother intuitively tried to prepare me for her death again, or a Higher Power did. I stood there holding the ticket, not understanding the message that day when I tried to give the ticket agent the information she requested. In my confusion that day, I couldn't even read the date printed on the ticket out loud. It was somehow stuck in my brain; but the meaning, at the time, meant nothing to me. Now I understood clearly for the first time. I held on to the receipt, my fingernails making indentations into the paper, feeling like I could crush it in my hands. It was then I realized, 'My God,' as my breath raced through my body, it was the **date my mother would die, the date of her death.**

Chapter 18

My father, the Reverend Norman Matthews, lived another ten years after the death of my mother. His life was a peaceful one, his children grown and gone, which I'm sure he really enjoyed, because that's how he preferred his life. If he had a choice: to be alone would be it. That life came abruptly to an end when my sister received a call from the minister at his church saying that our father didn't show up for service. He never missed a Sunday morning service and did not call anyone.

My brothers, Orlando, Norman and my sister, Yvonne, went to his home to look for him. The back door was ajar, but after looking through the house including the basement, there was no evidence of anyone in the house, nor had anyone been there.

They started checking the large backyard which our father made us clean and garden each week as children, passed the fishpond area, he called "a Dandy," and walked through the gate leading to the garage domain. My father rarely parked his car back there, too far from the front of the house. The area was supported by a small yard with rhubarb vegetables lining the alley fence. The threesome looked for my father, who was in his eighties.

They shouted, "Daddy, Daddy, where are you?" Just as they started to leave, a weak response barely floated on the breeze.

"I'm here," he said meekly, followed by a cough as he cleared his throat. Hearing the fragile sound, they followed the sound to a narrow area adjacent to the garage and fence line. They found our father on the ground, lodged between the garage and the wooden fence.

My brothers lifted him from his enclosure, moving fencing as necessary, and carried him into his home. Having spent the night outside, my siblings took him to the hospital for exposure. After leaving the hospital, my father stayed at Yvonne's home for his recuperation. He never returned to our 34th Street home. Over time, he became weaker.

I remember my telephone conversation with my father while he was in the hospital in Indianapolis. I was in Los Angeles, a school administrator.

"Hi Daddy."

"Well Beverley, it's good to hear your voice," my father said in a muffled phlegmy response.

Rightfully *Hers*

I could hear the smile in his voice and imagined his face brightening as he spoke to me.

"Well," I said, "how did it feel to sleep under the stars?" After all, how do you approach such an encounter. I knew how dreadful this experience had been for him. I never knew him to be an outdoorsman. Our family never went camping. The closest my father ever came to the outdoors was swimming in the ocean, and he was an excellent swimmer, powerful and strong. He should have been an Olympic swimmer in the breaststroke competition.

My father burst out laughing, then coughed and laughed again robustly.

"It wasn't too bad," he replied, while regaining his energy.

Months later, Yvonne called to tell me that our father didn't have much time to live, and he was asking for me. I made arrangements to visit him.

I flew in that Friday night. My father was so happy to see me. His face and his spirits lightened. We talked a little, like we had always been friends, which was never true, but he was always there as my father. He asked about my daughter Mia and my husband Clarence.

"Did your husband come with you?" His Jamaican accent still strong.

"No, not this time, Daddy," I said.

My father continued with questions about my school, etc.

I said to him, "Conserve your strength. We will talk again later."

My father looked at me intently. The corners of his mouth in a 'happy face.' He closed his hazel eyes and was immediately sound asleep.

The next day, I sat quietly with him as he dosed in and out of sleep.

The last time he awakened, he smiled again. "You still here?" His voice was fragile, but I recognized that he was assured of my presence.

I asked if he would like some hot tea. He nodded. I went to the kitchen to make a quick preparation. Upon return, I placed the cup at his lips, and he took a couple of sips. I wrapped my hands around his to steady his hands, felt his warm thin fingers, no longer fleshy, as he stared into my eyes. A rainbow held his features, comfortable, I would say content, as I looked into his face. I took the cup to the nearby kitchen and returned.

Rightfully *Hers*

I said, "Daddy," but he didn't open his eyes. I said his name again and took his hand. He was gone... quietly, peacefully.

***

Afterwards, my brother Norman called me the 'angel of death,' because both of our parents waited for me to come before they died. First my mother in 1988 and ten years later, my father. He would jokingly remark, "If anyone is ill, don't call Beverley!" Then he laughed, boisterously. Maybe he wasn't joking. I couldn't tell by looking into his eyes, wide, and playful. I didn't know what to say, when he made this comment more than once, while laughing and encouraging others to join in. I was immobilized. Each time I smiled, just to be part of the humor, never intending to be the butt of the joke. I didn't know how to respond. So, I said nothing.

***

I still have the red microfiber blanket the airlines presented to me after my mother's death. I thought it was a wool blend all those years, until I looked at the information on the tag. The tag said this fabric has self-extinguishing modacrylic fibers. One of these modern fabrics, manmade, probably filled with plastics; but I think not. It is soft and I guess good in times of a fire, a retardant. Interesting, my mother didn't need that.

Sometimes I throw it over myself, feeling my mother's presence, her comfort and warmth. Ironically, I had a vivid dream months after my mother's death. She was crying, as we sat quietly together.

I asked, "What's wrong Mother?"

"I'm looking for my mother," she said seemingly in desperation.

***

My mother was a beautiful person, inside and out. She should have had what was RIGHTFULLY HERS: a caring and loving mother, a husband who supported her fully and unconditionally; and children who loved her. I guess in the full scheme of life, Daphne received part. At 72 years old now, I realize that there are those who get very little in this world and/or give very little; and those whose abundance is cherished and compounded through small gifts given over time from the heartfelt passion of people who truly love them.

We stand together in our loss, our support, and in our love for each other; as we are fortified by the bonds that held us together.

In life and in death, my brothers, sisters, our father and even Phyllis, our grandmother, and all who loved my mother and were loved in turn by her, will stand in support of children who, like my mother, needed just a little support rightfully and freely given.

I imagined my mother as a child telling her story while sitting in the comfort of Grandam's cushioned lap. Her grandmother was gently patting her on the head and wiping Daphne's tears away as she said tenderly, "God bless you my child."

I felt that my mother rightfully deserved to be loved, cared for, sent to school, as well as surrounded by adults who valued her as a child, who listened to her, wanted to hear her questions, and embraced her when she was fearful; adults who made the world a better place for her. I felt these gifts were "Rightfully Hers."

In Memoriam

My mother, Daphne

My Family

My mother and father

My mother, Daphne in her 20s

Grandmother Phyllis 1980

Grandmother Phyllis 1970

Me, playing the Viola

My mother, Daphne

Aunt Phyllis

Me, at age 5

My brother, Norman

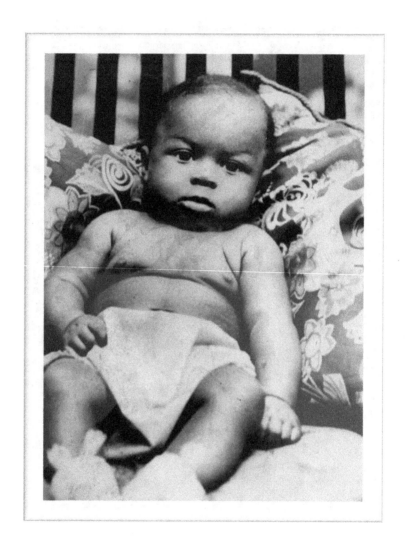

My brother, Orlando

My sister, Yvonne

My sister, Elaine

My brother, Eddie

My brother, Eddie & me

My father, Reverend Norman Matthews

Acknowledgements

I would like to acknowledge Dr. Clarence Clarkson, my husband, and my daughter, Mia Brown, Esq., for their endless support of my writing passion.

I would be remiss if I didn't thank Debra Funderburk of the Charlotte Writing Academy for her patience in helping me clarify my writings, while guiding me through the world of self-publishing.

About the Author

For 40 years, Beverley Clarkson was a teacher, school administrator and director of schools. Since retirement, she has pursued her lifelong passion of writing. Her first book, "It's of No Consequence," was greatly received and tore into the hearts of its readers. Comments attributed to this book include: "Amazing story, beautifully written;" "I was mesmerized and could not put it down;" "I just finished your book with tears in my eyes...."

Her new book, "Rightfully Hers," is the second book of a trilogy about her family. Beverley shares the stage of this book with her mother's writings from her childhood. Both women were born in Jamaica, B.W.I. and came to America when Beverley was a child. The author lived in Indiana and now resides in California. She is a graduate of Ball State University in Muncie, Indiana and received her master's degree from Pepperdine University in Los Angeles.

She is married to husband, Clarence, and they celebrated their 50th Wedding Anniversary on a Viking Cruise last year. Their daughter, son-in-law, Foreign Exchange daughter and family joined them in Spain for the beginning of this celebration. Two grandchildren, a niece in Los Angeles with a family in Atlanta, complete this union.

The author is currently working on her third book, "Hold on Kids," which will be published in 2021.

CPSIA information can be obtained
at www.ICGtesting.com
Printed in the USA
FSHW021953300320
68639FS

9 780578 659602